free~spirit SHAWLS

20 Eclectic Knits for Every Day

Lisa Shroyer

INTERWEAVE
interweave.com

Editor *Erica Smith*

Technical Editor *Therese Chynoweth*

Art Director *Liz Quan*

Photographer *Joe Hancock*

Photo Stylist *Emily Choi*

Illustrations *Kathie Kelleher*

Cover and Interior Design *Adrian Newman*

Production *Katherine Jackson*

Interweave
A division of F+W Media, Inc
201 East Fourth Street
Loveland, CO 80537
interweave.com

Manufactured in the USA by RR-Donnelley.

Library of Congress
Cataloging-in-Publication Data

Shroyer, Lisa.
 Free-spirit shawls : 20 eclectic knits for every
day / Lisa Shroyer.
     pages cm
ISBN 978-1-59668-904-6 (pbk.)
ISBN 978-1-59668-956-5 (PDF)
1. Knitting--Patterns. 2. Shawls. I. Title.
TT825.S539 2013
746.43'2--dc23

                                        2012033945

10 9 8 7 6 5 4 3 2

contents

introduction

The knitted shawl has become an icon in our strange little crafty world. What is it about this brief accessory, this slip of lace on the shoulders, this ever-morphing shape, that so enchants us?

As editor of *Knitscene*, I have seen my share of shawl designs. Shawl projects are a staple in the magazine, both because designers are always submitting interesting interpretations of them and because our readers love them so much. From this popularity came the idea to do a shawl book devoted to the triangles, semicircles, and rectangles that provide space for fun stitches, color play, and cool finishing treatments. I hope you enjoy the projects and tutorials in the book. May they take you to new heights of knitting expression!

Lisa Shroyer

size, style, and yarn

making and wearing modern shawls

This book is about knitting contemporary shawls and shawlettes—and incorporating fun techniques, quirky elements, and unusual yarns into your designs. The photography reflects my thinking about the shawl—as an accessory, it's feminine, bold, stylish, and versatile.

This is not a book about ethnic shawl traditions or heritage techniques. Many wonderful sources for this information are available, and I encourage you to do that research; it will enrich your knitting life. See page 132 for some recommendations.

You'll see that the shawls in this collection are organized by four themes: Color, Lace, Simplicity, and Texture.

- Color introduces stripes, slipped stitches, zigzags, and color-blocking—all manipulations of multiple colors in one project.

- Lace explores the endless possibilities rendered by the simple yet dramatic yarnover.

- Simplicity uses variegated yarns and simple stitches to create striking shawls that most knitters will find accessible.

- Finally, Texture takes on cables, knit-purl combinations, and the nubbly surfaces garter stitch can create.

Wearing Your Shawl

Let's talk about style. Many knitters enjoy knitting shawls but aren't quite sure how best to show them off. There are so many possible ways to wear your shawl, and it can be fun to experiment.

For smaller shawls: a shawl about 26" (66 cm) wide across the top edge makes a great kerchief. Simply hang the point in front and wrap the ends around the neck, knotting them in place—or bring the ends forward after wrapping them around the neck. Small and medium-sized shawls can also be wrapped around the shoulders off-center, so that the opening hits near the front of the shoulder. Knot the ends there or pin with a brooch.

For delicate lace or larger-sized shawls: Think about ensemble. A large "traditional" looking shawl doesn't have to look frumpy if you pair it with fresh styles and remember that it's an accessory. Use these shawls as part of your look— go Boho with torn denim, big jewelry, and flowy fabrics, or go dress-up with a slinky dress and dramatic earrings. A lace shawl can always be bundled and looped around the neck like a scarf. Though you won't see all the detail, the effect can still be striking.

Of course, almost all shawls can be worn traditionally, with the deepest part of the center straight down the back and the ends draped in front. You can wear sweet little semicircles and crescents this way and look very stylish today. Top a strapless dress with one and you have instant romance.

Side wrap. Pictured: Euclid (page 102).

Some shawl designs lend themselves to a tougher, more urban aesthetic. The projects in the Color chapter (see page 18) have this hip sensibility. Tuck a bold little shawl into the collar of a coat or leather jacket, bundle it like a cowl, grab your sunglasses, and you're ready for the city. Long, narrow shawls, such as Brome (see page 46) and The Return Journey (see page 116), can be worn like scarves, slung around the neck, or wrapped and tied.

Front knotted. Pictured: Mineral (page 34).

Kerchief, draped in front. Pictured: Basilica (page 20).

Side knotted. Pictured: Lindsay (page 82).

Traditional, draped over shoulders.
Pictured: Glen Lennox (page 112).

Superwash sock yarn also makes a great choice for a shawlette. Choose one phenomenal skein of yarn—perhaps hand-dyed—and get a full project out of it. Many popular designs both online and in this book are worked in fingering-weight yarn, which makes sock yarn an ideal substitute.

Choosing Your Yarn

Like scarves, shawls can be worn for warmth as much as for style. If you need a warm accessory, yarn choice is important. The projects in the Texture chapter (see page 100) are worked in heavier yarns with a lot of animal-fiber content. Bundle up in a long, cabled wrap and let the wind blow—you'll be cozy and comfortable. Shawls can be transeasonal as well—a silk laceweight yarn or superwash sock yarn can make spring and summer-ready wraps. Designs in the Lace chapter are well-suited to warm weather, but don't underestimate the potential warmth of a wool-silk blend in a fingering weight.

Each pattern in this book lists the actual yarn used, as well as the Craft Yarn Council of America's weight categorizations (yarnstandards.com). But because shawls don't need to fit or be any certain size, and gauge is in the eye of the beholder, you can switch any of the yarns to another weight. The size and drape of the piece will change, but that could create some cool effects. Always swatch with your proposed yarn and needles and compare your gauge to the pattern's. If you get fewer stitches/rows per inch than the pattern, your finished shawl will be larger than the sample. If you get more, your shawl will be smaller than the sample.

So get ready to cast on!

Chapter 2

shawl techniques

In this book, you'll discover many ways of making, shaping, and finishing shawls. Some methods are used again and again, while others are unique. In the following pages, we'll look at the basic construction methods and some typical techniques used in modern shawls.

The Top-Down Triangle

There are three main ways to knit a triangular shawl. One of the most popular is from the top down, with increases worked at four lines—one at each outer edge and two in the middle, each flanking the center spine. The standard top-down shawl begins with a garter tab, which is worked such that there is no visible cast-on; the shawl just grows from the top edge downward and outward.

Top-Down

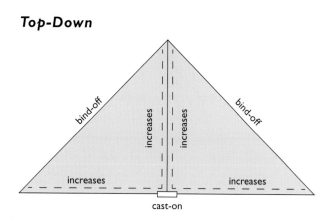

Three examples of top-down triangle shawls are Basilica (page 20), Spathe (above right; page 64), and Bryusa (below; page 78).

How to Work a Garter Tab

Using the invisible provisional cast-on (see Techniques), cast on 3 stitches. Knit 7 rows. Turn your work and use the right needle to pick up and knit 3 stitches down the side edge of the work. Unzip the provisional cast-on and place 3 live stitches on the left needle, then knit them, for a total of 9 stitches.

You now have a short piece of garter stitch with live stitches emerging from it on three sides. These three sections (of 3 stitches each) represent the three shaping "lanes" to be worked in the shawl body. After the cast-on, a standard shawl would be worked as follows: 3 garter stitches for the edging, yarnover increase, knit 1, yarnover, knit 1 (center spine), yarnover, knit 1, yarnover, 3 garter stitches for the edging.

As the stitches increase, patterning can be worked over the knit stitches. Each right-side row increases the stitch count by four, with the result that two triangles grow outward from the garter tab, with the center-spine knit stitch separating them down the middle. Obviously, the final rows and bind-off will be worked over many stitches. Top-down triangles can be small or large; just stop knitting when it suits you! Stitch patterns have to be worked in multiples that integrate with the rate of shaping and the stitch counts, but as you can see from Spathe (above), you can achieve beautiful allover patterns.

Other Triangles

The top-down is probably the most popular triangle construction method, but there are other ways to knit triangles. The bottom-up begins with a small cast-on and ends with a long bind-off edge (see diagram below). A wingspan-down triangle starts with a long cast-on that spans the width of the top edge and decreases at each edge down to the bottom point. And finally, a triangle can be worked side to side, with shaping at one edge to create the widening, then narrowing silhouette. We'll talk more about side to side shawls in the following section.

Elven (above; page 90) is not a true triangle, as it splits at the top to create wings, but its general shaping qualifies as bottom-up). Side to side shawls include Glen Lennox (page 112) and The Return Journey (page 116).

Wingspan-Down

← cast-on →

decreases

decreases

bind-off

Side to Side

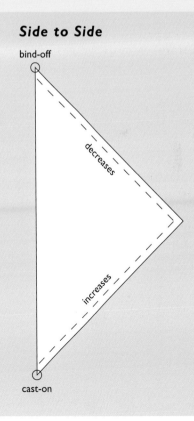

bind-off

decreases

increases

cast-on

Bottom-Up

bind-off

increases

increases

cast-on

Semicircles, Crescents, and Working Side to Side

Semicircles

Salter Path is worked from the top down, in growing half-rings of increases worked evenly across each row. Palmatum features the same shape and shaping arrangement as Salter Path, but Palmatum is worked from the bottom up, decreasing from the wide edge to the top.

Semicircle

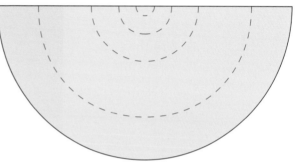

Crescents

Crescent shapes have a lot of flexibility. They can be short and deep with a strong upward curve or long and narrow with a slight upward curve. Brome is long and narrow, almost scarflike, with its 75" (190.5 cm) length and (at its widest) 12" (30.5 cm) depth. This shawl begins at the wide bottom edge and, after the lace section, is shaped with short-rows worked within garter stitch, which creates a slight curvilinear profile. Lindsay features this same bottom-up short-row construction. It is almost as long and narrow as Brome, but in a lighter yarn, which doesn't create the same heavy scarf look.

Bethe is a small crescent with a more pronounced roundness. The garter-stitch body is worked first, side to side, with increases at the outer edge to create both the shape and a pick-up for the edging. This style of construction is specific to the Shetland tradition. See page 58 for more information on the technique.

Salter Path (above; page 24), Brome (page 46), Palmatum (page 50), Bethe (page 54), Lindsay (page 82), and Rhoeas (page 94) are semicircles and crescents.

Many projects in this book use short-rows, but they achieve quite different results in each design. At the most basic, a short-row creates added depth in an isolated section of knitting. If you have 15 stitches and work a short-row across only 7 stitches, those 7 stitches will have 2 more rows worked than the surrounding stitches (the right-side row, then returning wrong-side row). You can see how short-rows add up to make curved shapes, with the center fabric deeper than the ends, which is ideal for crescent shawls. See Techniques for instructions on how to work in short-rows.

NOTE: Not all short-rows require wrapping the turning stitch. In garter stitch and other stitch patterns, the gap at the turn won't show. You can simply turn and continue working. Individual patterns will explain how to work their short-rows.

Brome (above; page 46). Bethe (bottom right; page 54).

Working Side to Side

Shawls with rounded silhouettes can be worked from side to side. This approach usually requires casting on a few stitches, then increasing evenly to the full depth, then decreasing back to the other end. The shaping can be worked solely at the outer edge or across the width of each row. Conversely, you can cast on the full number of stitches and create the shape with short-rows (above right).

As previously mentioned, you can also work triangles side to side. By adjusting the rate of shaping, a sideways triangle can be short and deep or long and narrow. The Return Journey only increases (and then decreases) every fourth row, creating a long and shallow shape. The shaping is worked at the right-hand edge, allowing new repeats of the stitch pattern to be added every few inches. Glen Lennox features a more familiar triangular shape, measuring 55" (139.5 cm) wide at the top edge and 16½" (42 cm) deep at the center point. The increases (and then decreases) are worked every right-side row, so the shaping occurs twice as fast as in The Return Journey. In Rhoeas, by working side to side, the knitter can create a fringed edge as the shawl is knitted. See page 98 for more about this technique and how it suits sideways triangles.

Cast-Ons and Bind-Offs for Shawls

Each pattern in this book will recommend specific techniques for casting on and binding off. But here are a few things to keep in mind when you knit shawls:

1. The edges should be elastic, so avoid working too tightly when you cast on and bind off. When it's blocked, your shawl will likely stretch and grow quite a bit. The edges will need to stretch and grow with the overall fabric.

2. You should become familiar with provisional cast-ons, especially when you work top-down triangles. See the Techniques section for instructions.

When you bind off a large number of stitches, consider using two circular needles. You'll be able to spread the knitting out and methodically work a loose bind-off with consistent tension.

For lace projects, in addition to working loosely when casting on and binding off, you can also choose specific techniques that are looser than the standard (long-tail) cast-on and bind-off. See the Techniques section at the back of the book for more information on these methods.

Cast-ons: Backward-loop cast-on, Knitted cast-on.

Bind-offs: Decrease bind-off.

Palmatum (page 50).

Make It Pretty: Finishing Tips
Weaving in Ends

Even if there is a definite right and wrong side to your shawl, a shawl is functionally a reversible project. Because people will see the wrong side, you should endeavor to weave in ends neatly. Consider these tips:

1. Join new balls a couple of inches in from the outer edge. This way, there won't be a knot or loose end right at the edge of the project.

2. Leave long tails and weave in the end for an inch more than you would in a normal project. See 4, below, for why.

3. Use duplicate stitch to weave in ends on the wrong side. If the project is worked in stockinette, then work reverse stockinette duplicate on the wrong side, tucked into the plainer areas of knitting (not through lace, for instance). If the project is worked in a combination of stitches, limit the weaving in to a consistent area and mimic that stitch in duplicate. If the project is worked in garter stitch, use garter-stitch duplicate (*See the Techniques section on page 125 for more information on how to work these forms of duplicate stitch*).

4. Weave in ends before blocking, but wait to trim the tails until after blocking. Stretching the fabric out will cause the tails to recede into the fabric, affecting the length of the end to be trimmed.

Rhoeas (page 94).

Blocking

Blocking is probably the most important step in shawl knitting. To achieve clean edges and ideal stretch across the fabric, use blocking wires or cotton string threaded evenly through the edges and stretched taut to create a kind of blocking wire. You will need T-pins to hold the wires in place. Your project may also require T-pins to shape out a scalloped edge. However, don't use T-pins to create the straight edges; they will create unintentional scalloping.

Try using Wool Wash to wet-block your shawl, especially if it predominantly features lace. You want to really stretch lace fabric to its fullest extent to flatten the stitches and open the pattern. Soaking lace will help with this stretching. Heavier knits, such as the worsted-weight cabled shawls in the Texture chapter, don't require this kind of aggressive blocking. For The Return Journey, I pinned the shawl flat, misted it with clean water, and then ironed the three points (over a damp towel) to really flatten them. Always read your yarn label before blocking. If it contains synthetic content, ironing may not be a good idea. Superwash wools tend to lose body when wetted, but this may not matter with a shawl. Remember, to get an accurate gauge from your initial swatch, you should block and treat the swatch the same way you will treat the finished shawl.

Even After It's All Knitted and Done

After you block your finished shawl, you may want to periodically reblock it. With wear and use, the shape may start to shrink back to its original dimensions. Lace may close up; you may find that the fabric wrinkles when left wadded in the backseat of your car. Washing and blocking will bring the life back to the knitting. And doing so may just reignite your passion for shawls all over again—taking you down the road to your next favorite project.

color

Use multiple colors to create bold, alluring shawls. From mosaic colorwork to stripes, from chevrons to color-blocking, these designs combine hues and strong graphic elements for dramatic impact.

Hilary Smith Callis

FINISHED SIZE

About 54" (137 cm) wide at top edge and 13¾" (35 cm) deep.

YARN

Fingering weight (#1 Super Fine).

Shown here: Brooklyn Tweed Loft (100% wool; 275 yd [251 m]/50 g): #21 Hayloft (MC) and #23 Fossil (CC), 1 skein each.

NEEDLES

Size U.S. 5 (3.75 mm): 29" (74 cm) or longer circular (cir).

Adjust needle size if necessary to obtain the correct gauge.

NOTIONS

Tapestry needle.

GAUGE

22 stitches and 26 rows = 4" (10 cm) in stockinette stitch; 23 stitches and 44 rows = 4" (10 cm) in pattern stitch.

Mosaic colorwork creates the allover graphic design in this easy-to-knit stylish shawlette. The triangle builds from the bottom up with yarnovers at each edge. A rustic wool fingering-weight yarn adds airy warmth to a sleek design.

Notes

🖋 This shawl is worked in a slipped-stitch pattern, which means that only one color is worked per row and colors are switched every two rows. When you change colors, be sure to bring the new yarn in front of the yarn you were just working with before you begin the next row.

🖋 In the Set-up and Body charts, note that the even-numbered (wrong-side) rows are worked in the same pattern as the odd-numbered (right-side) rows that precede them. You can work these rows without looking at the chart. Simply purl all stitches that are the same color as your working yarn (with the exception of the yarnovers and two stitches knitted at each edge) and slip all stitches in the other color. In the even-numbered rows of the Edging chart, knit all stitches that are the same color as your working yarn and slip all stitches that are the other color.

Shawl

With MC, CO 2 sts.

ROWS 1 AND 2: With MC, knit.

ROWS 3 AND 4: With CC, knit.

ROWS 5 AND 6: With MC, knit.

ROW 7: With CC, k2, yo, rotate piece 90 degrees clockwise and pick up and knit 3 sts along edge (1 st for each garter ridge), yo, rotate piece 90 degrees clockwise and pick up and knit 2 sts along CO edge—9 sts.

ROW 8: With CC, k2, yo, purl to last 2 sts, yo, k2—11 sts.

Beg with MC, work Rows 1–12 of Set-up chart—35 sts. Work Rows 1–24 of Body chart 5 times, then Rows 1–12 only—299 sts. Work Rows 1–5 of Edging chart—309 sts.

Note: Edging chart is the same as Rows 13–17 of Body chart, but all sts not slipped are knitted instead of purled on Rows 14 and 16.

NEXT ROW: With MC, BO all sts kwise.

Finishing

Weave in all ends. Block piece to finished measurements, taking care to pin the bottom edge in a rounded shape.

Set-up

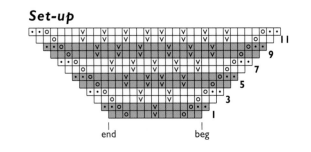

end   beg

Body

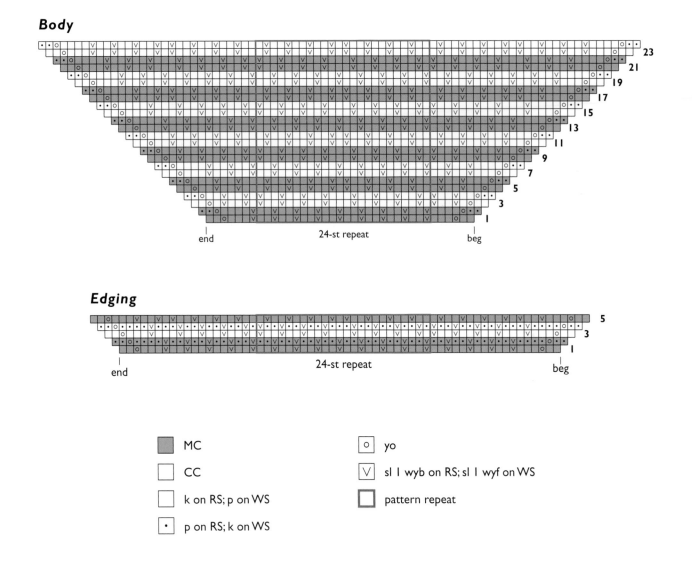

end   24-st repeat   beg

Edging

end   24-st repeat   beg

MC

CC

k on RS; p on WS

• p on RS; k on WS

○ yo

∨ sl 1 wyb on RS; sl 1 wyf on WS

pattern repeat

salter path

Melissa J. Goodale

FINISHED SIZE

About 52" (132 cm) wide at top edge and 26" (66 cm) deep.

YARN

Fingering weight (#1 Super Fine).

Shown here: Hazel Knits Artisan Sock (90% wool, 10% nylon; 400 yd [366 m]/120 g): Low Tide (MC), Fudge (CC1), and Beach Glass (CC2), 1 skein each.

NEEDLES

Size U.S. 6 (4 mm): 24" (60 cm) circular (cir).

Adjust needle size if necessary to obtain the correct gauge.

NOTIONS

Tapestry needle.

GAUGE

24 stitches and 32 rows = 4" (10 cm) in stockinette stitch; 22 stitches and 27 rows = 4" (10 cm) in garter stitch.

This shawl uses the formulas for a full-circle shawl and adapts them to create a semicircle. You'll find Melissa's tutorial on this construction on page 29. Inspired by waves washing over the rocks of a tide pool, the color changes in the finished shawl are visually striking, as is the transition from garter stitch to lace.

Shawl

With CC1, using the Emily Ocker circular beginning (see Techniques and Note), CO 10 sts. Cont with CC1.

NEXT ROW: Sl 1 with yarn in front (wyf), k7, sl 1 wyf, k1, turn.

NEXT ROW: Sl 1 wyf, k1, [k1f&b] 5 times, k1, sl 1 wyf, k1, turn—15 sts.

Arc 1

ROWS 1–3: Sl 1 wyf, k12, sl 1 wyf, k1.

ROW 4: Sl 1 wyf, k1, [k1f&b] 10 times, k1, sl 1 wyf, k1—25 sts.

Arc 2

ROWS 1–5: Sl 1 wyf, k22, sl 1 wyf, k1.

ROW 6: Sl 1 wyf, k1, [k1f&b] 20 times, k1, sl 1 wyf, k1—45 sts.

Arc 3

ROWS 1–11: Sl 1 wyf, k42, sl 1 wyf, k1.

ROW 12: Sl 1 wyf, k1, [k1f&b] 40 times, k1, sl 1 wyf, k1—85 sts.

Arc 4

Change to MC.

ODD ROWS 1–23: Sl 1 wyf, k1, [sl 1 wyf, k4] 16 times, [sl 1 wyf] 2 times, k1.

EVEN ROWS 2–22: Sl 1 wyf, k1, [k1tbl, k4] 16 times, k1tbl, sl 1 wyf, k1.

ROW 24: Sl 1 wyf, k1, [k1tbl, M1, (k1f&b) 4 times] 16 times, k1tbl, sl 1 wyf, k1—165 sts.

Arc 5

ODD ROWS 1–47: Sl 1 wyf, k1, [sl 1 wyf, k9] 16 times, [sl 1 wyf] 2 times, k1.

EVEN ROWS 2–46: Sl 1 wyf, k1, [k1tbl, k9] 16 times, k1tbl, sl 1 wyf, k1.

ROW 48: Sl 1 wyf, k1, [k1tbl, M1, (k1f&b) 9 times] 16 times, k1tbl, sl 1 wyf, k1—325 sts.

Lace

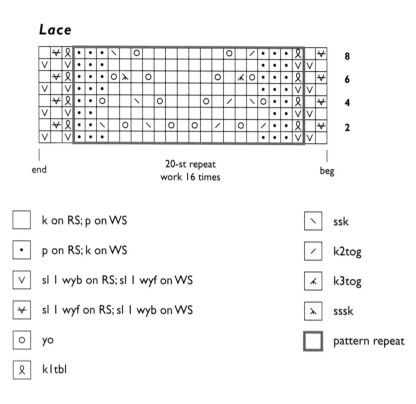

20-st repeat
work 16 times

end   beg

	k on RS; p on WS		ssk
	p on RS; k on WS		k2tog
	sl 1 wyb on RS; sl 1 wyf on WS		k3tog
	sl 1 wyf on RS; sl 1 wyb on WS		sssk
	yo		pattern repeat
	k1tbl		

Arc 6

ODD ROWS 1–23: Sl 1 wyf, k1, [sl 1 wyf, k19] 16 times, [sl 1 wyf] 2 times, k1.

EVEN ROWS 2–24: Sl 1 wyf, k1, [k1tbl, k19] 16 times, k1tbl, sl 1 wyf, k1.

Lace Section

With CC2, work Rows 1–8 of Lace chart 6 times.

NEXT ROW: With MC, sl 1 wyf, k1, purl to last 2 sts, sl 1 wyf, k1.

NEXT ROW: Sl 1 wyf, knit to last 2 sts, sl 1 wyf, k1.

Rep last row twice more.

NEXT ROW: With CC1, sl 1 wyf, knit to last 2 sts, sl 1 wyf, k1.

Rep last row twice more.

BO ALL STS AS FOLL: *K2tog, slip rem st back to left needle; rep from * until 1 st rem; fasten off last st.

Finishing

Weave in all ends. Block piece to finished measurements.

The Anatomy of

semicircular shawls

Melissa J. Goodale

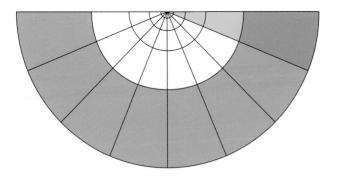

Parts of a semicircular shawl: wedges (yellow) and arcs (blue)

Semicircular shawls are flattering and easy to wear. Because they are created using a basic mathematical formula, they are also straightforward to design and a wonderful way to play with stitch patterns. When you create a semicircular shawl, it's best to think of the design in terms of three elements: the top edging, the wedges, and the arcs.

The top edging is created by the first and last stitches in each row. These do not count when you calculate the increase math and can be greater than one stitch wide. In the Salter Path, the edge stitches are two stitches wide on one side and three stitches wide on the other. The wedges (shaded in yellow) are a fixed width in each arc (shaded in blue). The width of the wedge determines the stitch count of the stitch pattern that can be repeated across the design. The height of the arc will determine the row count of the stitch pattern that can be used in that arc.

The math used to create the design is straightforward. At the end of each arc, double the stitch count in the row (not including the decorative edge stitches). Each arc will have twice the row count of the arc before it. Cast on, double the stitch count in Row 2, double the stitch count in Row 4, double the stitch count in Row 8, et cetera. This method makes incorporating stitch patterns easy because the counts stay fixed for a set number of rows. There's no need to figure out what to do with extra stitches created in every or every other row, as there is with so many other shapes.

FINISHED SIZE

About 48" (122 cm) wide and 13" (33 cm) deep.

YARN

Fingering Weight (#1 Super Fine).

Shown here: Claudia Hand Painted Yarn Fingering Weight (100% merino; 175 yd [160 m]/50 g): Aubergine (MC) and Marigold (CC), 2 skeins each.

NEEDLES

Size U.S. 5 (3.75 mm): 24" (60 cm) circular (cir).

Adjust needle size if necessary to obtain the correct gauge.

NOTIONS

Tapestry needle.

GAUGE

20 stitches and 50 rows = 4" (10 cm) in beehive stitch.

This unisex design, with its architectural elements, is a sharp contrast to the softer connotations of "shawl." Bold stripes are emphasized by the texture of beehive stitch, while an asymmetrical structure creates its own interest.

❧ This shawl is worked in two halves. The horizontal stripes are worked first, increasing on both sides along the left side. Stitches are then picked up to make the second half of vertical stripes, decreasing only on the right side.

STITCH GUIDE

Beehive Stitch (beg on the WS)

ROWS 1, 2, AND 4: Purl.

ROWS 3, 5, AND 6: Knit.

Repeat Rows 1–6 for pattern.

Shawl

Horizontal Stripe Half

With MC, CO 1 st.

ROW 1: (RS) P1f&b—2 sts.

ROW 2: (WS) K1f&b, k1—3 sts.

ROW 3: Purl to last st, p1f&b—4 sts.

ROW 4: K1f&b, knit to end—5 sts.

ROW 5: Knit to last st, k1f&b—6 sts.

Cont to inc 1 st at left-hand edge on every row, work Rows 1–6 of beehive st (see Stitch Guide). *With CC, work 2 reps of beehive st. With MC, work 2 reps of beehive st. Rep from * 5 times more—156 sts. BO all sts.

Vertical Stripe Half

With RS facing and MC, pick up and knit 80 sts evenly along right-hand edge (unshaped selvedge) of first half.

ROWS 1 AND 3: (WS) Knit.

ROW 2: (RS) P2tog, purl to end—1 st dec'd.

ROW 4: K2tog, knit to end—1 st dec'd.

Cont to dec at beg of RS rows, work 1 rep of beehive st. *With CC, work 2 reps of beehive st.

With MC, work 2 reps of beehive st. Rep from * until 1 st rem. Fasten off last st.

Finishing

Weave in all ends. Block piece to finished measurements.

mineral

Rosemary (Romi) Hill

FINISHED SIZE

About 13" (33 cm) deep and 47" (119.5 cm) long.

YARN

Fingering weight (#1 Super Fine).

Shown here: Anzula Sebastian (70% superwash merino, 30% sea cell; 395 yd [361 m]/115 g): Shiitake (A) and Clay (B), 1 skein each.

NEEDLES

Size U.S. 5 (3.75 mm).

Adjust needle size if necessary to obtain the correct gauge.

NOTIONS

Markers (m); blocking wires; T-pins.

GAUGE

21 stitches and 30 rows = 4" (10 cm) in garter stitch, after blocking.

Worked side to side with shaping and short-rows, this subtle shawl features a curved shape and pebbly textures. In two colors of a sea-cell blend yarn, it makes a great transeasonal accessory that wraps beautifully.

🍃 You will change colors frequently in this project; carry the unused color up along the side as you work.

STITCH GUIDE

Twist 2 (T2)

Bring the right needle behind first st on the left needle and knit the 2nd st on the left needle through the back loop (tbl); knit the first st tbl and drop both sts from the needle, pulling the sts tight.

Shawl

Increase section

With A, use the knitted method (see Techniques) to CO 25 sts (counts as Row 1).

ROW 2: Knit all sts through the back loop (tbl).

Change to B.

ROW 3: K1tbl, knit to last st, k1tbl.

ROW 4: Yo, k1tbl, knit to last st, k1tbl—1 st inc'd.

Change to A.

ROW 5: K1tbl, knit to last st, k1tbl.

Beg working in short-rows (see Techniques) as foll:

ROW 6: Yo, k1tbl, k13, place marker (pm), knit to last 2 sts, wrap next st, turn; k1tbl, knit to m, sl m, k3, BO 8 sts (first st BO will be from 2 sts already on right needle), k4, k1tbl, (6 sts on needle after BO), turn, cont as foll:

[k1tbl, k4, k1tbl, turn] 7 times,

CO 8 sts with the knitted method, turn,

k1tbl, sl m, k9, wrap next st, turn,

k1tbl, knit to m, remove m, T2 (see Stitch Guide), [k1tbl] to end,

k1tbl, knit to last st, k1tbl—1 st inc'd.

Change to B.

ROW 7: K1tbl, knit to last st, k1tbl.

ROW 8: Yo, k1tbl, knit to last st, k1tbl—1 st inc'd.

Change to A.

ROW 9: K1tbl, knit to last st, k1tbl.

ROW 10: Yo, k1tbl, knit to last st, k1tbl—1 st inc'd.

Work Rows 3–10 eight more times—61 sts.

Change to B.

ROW 11: K1tbl, knit to last st, k1tbl.

ROW 12: Yo, k1tbl, knit to last st, k1tbl—1 st inc'd.

Change to A.

ROW 13: K1tbl, knit to last st, k1tbl.

ROW 14: Yo, k1tbl, k13, pm, k43, wrap next st, turn; k1tbl, knit to m, sl m, k3, BO 8 sts (first st BO will be from 2 sts already on right needle), k4, k1tbl (6 sts on needle after BO), turn; cont as foll:

[k1tbl, k4, k1tbl, turn] 7 times,

CO 8 sts with the knitted method, turn,

k1tbl, sl m, k9, wrap next st, turn,

k1tbl, knit to m, remove m, T2, [k1tbl] to end,

k1tbl, knit to last st, k1tbl—1 st inc'd.

Change to B.

ROW 15: K1tbl, knit to last st, k1tbl.

ROW 16: Yo, k1tbl, knit to last st, k1tbl—1 st inc'd.

Change to A.

ROW 17: K1tbl, knit to last st, k1tbl.

ROW 18: Yo, k1tbl, knit to last st, k1tbl—1 st inc'd.

Work Rows 11–18 one more time—69 sts.

Middle section

Change to B.

ROWS 19 AND 20: K1tbl, knit to last st, k1tbl.

Change to A.

ROW 21: K1tbl, knit to last st, k1tbl.

ROW 22: K1tbl, k14, pm, k40 (it may be helpful to use a marker here), wrap next st, turn; k1tbl, knit to m, sl m, k3, BO 8 sts (first st BO will be from 2 sts already on right needle), k4, k1tbl (6 sts on needle after BO), turn; cont as foll:

[k1tbl, k4, k1tbl, turn] 7 times,

CO 8 sts with the knitted method, turn,

k1tbl, sl m, k9, wrap next st, turn,

k1tbl, knit to m, remove m, T2, [k1tbl] to end,

k1tbl, knit to last st, k1tbl.

Change to B.

ROWS 23 AND 24: K1tbl, knit to last st, k1tbl.

Change to A.

ROWS 25 AND 26: K1tbl, knit to last st, k1tbl.

Work Rows 19–25 twenty-one more times. The piece should measure about 34¼" (87 cm) from CO along straight edge.

Transition section

Change to B.

ROWS 27 AND 28: K1tbl, knit to last st, k1tbl.

Change to A.

ROW 29: K1tbl, knit to last st, k1tbl.

ROW 30: K1tbl, k14, pm, k40 (it may be helpful to place a marker here), wrap next st, turn; k1tbl, knit to m, sl m, k3, BO 8 sts (first st BO will be from 2 sts already on right needle), k4, k1tbl (6 sts on needle after BO), turn; cont as foll:

[k1tbl, k4, k1tbl, turn] 7 times,

CO 8 sts with the knitted method, turn,

k1tbl, sl m, k9, wrap next st, turn,

k1tbl, knit to m, remove m, T2, [k1tbl] to end,

k1tbl, knit to last st, k1tbl.

Change to B.

ROWS 31 AND 32: K1tbl, knit to last st, k1tbl.

Decrease section

Change to A.

ROW 33: K1tbl, knit to last st, k1tbl.

ROW 34: K2tog tbl, knit to last st, k1tbl—1 st dec'd.

Change to B.

ROW 35: K1tbl, knit to last st, k1tbl.

ROW 36: K2tog tbl, knit to last st, k1tbl—1 st dec'd.

Change to A.

ROW 37: K1tbl, knit to last st, k1tbl.

ROW 38: K1tbl, k14, pm, k9, wrap next st, turn, k1tbl, knit to m, sl m, k3, BO 8 sts (first st BO will be from 2 sts already on right needle), k4, k1tbl (6 sts on needle after BO), turn; cont as foll:

[k1tbl, k4, k1tbl, turn] 7 times,

CO 8 sts with the knitted method, turn,

k1tbl, sl m, k43, wrap next st, turn,

k1tbl, knit to m, remove m, T2, [k1tbl] to end,

k2tog tbl, knit to last st, k1tbl—1 st dec'd.

Change to B.

ROW 39: K1tbl, knit to last st, k1tbl.

ROW 40: K2tog tbl, k1tbl, knit to last st, k1tbl—1 st dec'd.

Work Rows 33–40 once more—61 sts rem.

Change to A.

ROW 41: K1tbl, knit to last st, k1tbl.

ROW 42: K2tog tbl, knit to last st, k1tbl—1 st dec'd.

Change to B.

ROW 43: K1tbl, knit to last st, k1tbl.

ROW 44: K2tog tbl, knit to last st, k1tbl—1 st dec'd.

Change to A.

ROW 45: K1tbl, knit to last st, k1tbl.

ROW 46: K1tbl, k14, pm, k9, wrap next st, turn, k1tbl, knit to m, sl m, k3, BO 8 sts (first st BO will be from 2 sts already on right needle), k4, k1tbl (6 sts on needle after BO), turn; cont as foll:

[k1tbl, k4, k1tbl, turn] 7 times,

CO 8 sts with the knitted method, turn,

k1tbl, sl m, knit to last 2 sts,

wrap next st, turn,

k1tbl, knit to m, remove m, T2, [k1tbl] to end,

k2tog tbl, knit to last st, k1tbl—1 st dec'd.

Change to B.

ROW 47: K1tbl, knit to last st, k1tbl.

ROW 48: K2tog tbl, k1tbl, knit to last st, k1tbl—1 st dec'd.

Work Rows 41–48 eight more times—25 sts rem.

Change to A.

ROW 49: K1tbl, knit to last st, k1tbl.

ROW 50: K2tog tbl, BO all sts.

Finishing

Weave in all ends. Wash using Wool Wash and use blocking wires and pins to pin out stripes into points at bottom edge of shawl.

cimarron

Alexis Winslow

FINISHED SIZE
About 58" (147.5 cm) wide 27" (68.5 cm) deep, not including fringe.

YARN
Sport weight (#2 Fine).

Shown here: Louet Gems Sport Weight (100% merino; 225 yd [205 m]/100g): #01 Champagne (MC), 2 skeins; #47 Terra cotta (CC1) and #53 Caribou (CC2), 1 skein each.

NEEDLES
Size U.S. 7 (4.5 mm): 24" (60 cm) circular.

Adjust needle size if necessary to obtain the correct gauge.

NOTIONS
Markers (m); ruler; size K/10.5 (6.5 mm) crochet hook; tapestry needle.

GAUGE
18½ sts and 28 rows = 4" (10 cm) in stockinette stitch, after blocking.

Built-in fringe and zigzags of color make for a striking and playful shawlette. Worked in a Southwestern palette, Alexis Winslow's design has a unisex quality that makes it ideal for urban gents and bold ladies alike.

❦ The fringe is created as the shawl is knitted. At the beginning of each row, measure out 12" (30.5 cm) of the working yarn. Fold this length of yarn in half, making a loop of yarn 6" (15 cm) long, and firmly knot it at the base right by the selvedge edge. Begin knitting normally, leaving the loop to dangle as you work. On rows in which you're changing color, break the yarn for the old color leaving a 6" (15 cm) tail, and join the new color at the side, also leaving a 6" (15 cm) tail. Then knot the two together as you did for the loops.

STITCH GUIDE

S2KP

Slip 2 sts tog as if to k2tog, k1, pass 2 slipped sts over—2 sts dec'd.

Shawl

With CC1, CO 26 sts. See Note about working fringe at beg of rows.

ROW 1: (WS) K2, place marker (pm), knit to last 2 sts, pm, k2.

ROW 2: (RS) Knit to 1 st before m, k1f&b, pass marker, *k1f&b, k9, s2kp (see Stitch Guide), k8, k1f&b (ending at m); rep from * to last m, k1f&b, knit to end—2 sts inc'd.

NOTE: On Rows 2–20, there is no repeat.

ROW 3: (WS) Purl.

ROW 4: (RS) Rep Row 2—2 sts inc'd.

ROW 5: (WS) Knit.

ROW 6: (RS) Change to MC and rep Row 2—2 sts inc'd.

ROW 7: (WS) Purl.

ROW 8: (RS) With CC1, rep Row 2—2 sts inc'd.

ROW 9: (WS) Knit.

ROW 10: (RS) With MC, rep Row 2—2 sts inc'd.

ROW 11: (WS) Purl.

ROW 12: (RS) With CC1, rep Row 2—2 sts inc'd.

ROW 13: (WS) Knit.

ROW 14: (RS) With MC, rep Row 2—2 sts inc'd.

ROW 15: (WS) Purl.

ROW 16: (RS) Rep Row 2—2 sts inc'd.

ROW 17: (WS) Purl.

ROW 18: (RS) Rep Row 2—2 sts inc'd.

ROW 19: (WS) Purl to end, break yarn, leaving a 6" (15 cm) tail.

ROW 20: (RS) With CC2, CO 13 sts onto free needle then use this needle to knit across row, then use the backward-loop method (see Techniques) to CO 13 sts at end of row—70 sts.

ROWS 21–39: Rep Rows 1–19, using CC2 when CC is called for—88 sts.

ROW 40: (RS) With CC, CO 13 sts, knit to end, CO 13 sts—114 sts.

Rep Rows 1–40 twice more—290 sts. Rep Rows 1–14 once—304 sts.

NEXT ROW: (WS) Knit.

NEXT ROW: (RS) Rep Row 2—2 sts inc'd.

Rep last 2 rows once more—308 sts.

NEXT ROW: Knit.

BO all sts very loosely.

Finishing

Wet-block the shawl, stretching it to the finished measurements. Smooth out the fringe so that it dries straight and flat. Let the shawl dry completely before moving it. The shawl is expected to relax and shrink a bit after blocking. Gather each fringe section into two bunches. Make each bunch into a tassel by tying the strands together in a big knot at the base by the selvedge, as shown on opposite page. Add an extra tassel to the tip of the triangle: With six 12" (30.5 cm) lengths of CC1 held together, fold the cord in half to form a long loop. With a crochet hook, draw the loop through the tip of the shawl. Pull the ends of the loop through the eye of the loop to form the tassel. Trim all the loops to the same length, about 3" (7.5 cm) from their base.

lace

Romance and whimsy meet in the modern lace shawl. These designs nod to knitting's history while bringing the yarnover firmly into the twenty-first century. Choose chunky yarns for high-impact lace or lighter weight yarns and allover patterning for a more traditional look.

brome

Alexandra Beck

FINISHED SIZE

About 80" (203 cm) wide and 12" (30.5 cm) deep.

YARN

Heavy worsted weight (#4 Medium).

Shown here: Schoppel Wolle In-Silk (75% merino, 25% silk; 219 yd [200 m]/100g): #6051 Parsley, 3 skeins.

Yarn distributed by Skacel.

NEEDLES

Cast-on—Size U.S. 10½ (7 mm): 40" (100 cm) circular (cir).

Body—Size U.S. 8 (5 mm): 40" (100 cm) cir.

Adjust needle size if necessary to obtain the correct gauge.

NOTIONS

Tapestry needle.

GAUGE

11 stitches and 19½ rows = 4" (10 cm) in lace patt on smaller needles; 12 stitches and 36 rows = 4" (10 cm) in garter stitch on smaller needles.

For this shawl, the short-row crescent is stretched into scarf-like proportions. A wide lace border transitions into a narrow garter-stitch body in which short-rows create subtle curvilinear shaping. Worked in a chunky-weight wool-silk blend, Brome makes for quick knitting; yet its intricacy makes it decidedly appealing.

NOTES

🌿 This shawl is worked from the bottom up and shaped with short-rows.

🌿 Within the lace pattern, stitch counts will vary from row to row.

🌿 The first and last three stitches of each row are worked in garter stitch. These stitches are shown on the chart, outside the repeat box.

🌿 Because the body is worked in garter stitch, you do not need to hide the short-row wraps.

Shawl

Lace border

With larger needles and using a stretchy CO (see page 125 for tips), CO 240 sts. Change to smaller needles and knit 2 rows. Work Rows 1–34 of the Lace chart, working the edges in garter st (see Notes) and repeating the 18-st rep across the interior sts.

Body

Knit 2 rows, then work short-rows (see Techniques) as follows:

ROW 1: (RS) K127, wrap next st, turn.

ROW 2: (WS) K14, wrap next st, turn.

ROW 3: K21, wrap next st, turn.

ROW 4: K28, wrap next st, turn.

ROW 5: K35, wrap next st, turn.

ROW 6: K42, wrap next st, turn.

ROW 7: K49, wrap next st, turn.

ROW 8: K56, wrap next st, turn.

ROW 9: K63, wrap next st, turn.

ROW 10: K70, wrap next st, turn.

ROW 11: K77, wrap next st, turn.

ROW 12: K84, wrap next st, turn.

ROW 13: K91, wrap next st, turn.

ROW 14: K98, wrap next st, turn.

ROW 15: K104, wrap next st, turn.

ROW 16: K110, wrap next st, turn.

ROW 17: K116, wrap next st, turn.

ROW 18: K122, wrap next st, turn.

ROW 19: K128, wrap next st, turn.

ROW 20: K134, wrap next st, turn.

ROW 21: K140, wrap next st, turn.

ROW 22: K146, wrap next st, turn.

ROW 23: K152, wrap next st, turn.

Lace

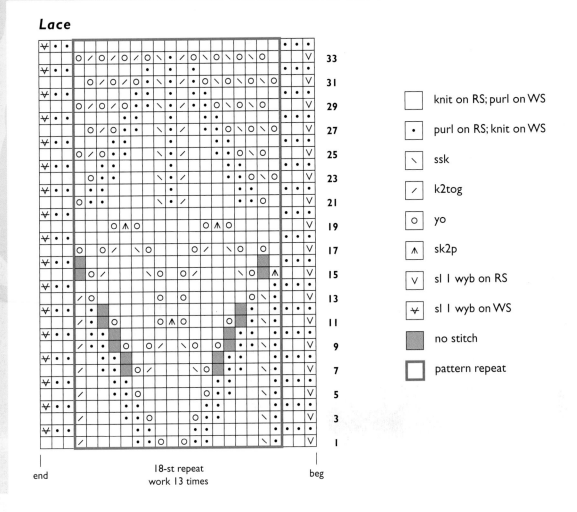

end

18-st repeat
work 13 times

beg

☐	knit on RS; purl on WS
•	purl on RS; knit on WS
＼	ssk
／	k2tog
O	yo
∧	sk2p
V	sl 1 wyb on RS
⩡	sl 1 wyb on WS
▨	no stitch
☐	pattern repeat

ROW 24: K158, wrap next st, turn.

ROW 25: K164, wrap next st, turn.

ROW 26: K170, wrap next st, turn.

ROW 27: K175, wrap next st, turn.

ROW 28: K180, wrap next st, turn.

ROW 29: K185, wrap next st, turn.

ROW 30: K190, wrap next st, turn.

ROW 31: K195, wrap next st, turn.

ROW 32: K200, wrap next st, turn.

ROW 33: K205, wrap next st, turn.

ROW 34: K210, wrap next st, turn.

ROW 35: K215, wrap next st, turn.

ROW 36: K220, wrap next st, turn.

ROW 37: K225, wrap next st, turn.

ROW 38: K230, wrap next st, turn.

ROW 39: Knit to end of row.

ROW 40: (WS) Knit to end of row.

BO all sts.

Finishing

Weave in all ends. Block piece to finished measurements.

palmatum

Kyoko Nakayoshi

FINISHED SIZE

About 43" (109 cm) wide and 19½" (49.5 cm) deep.

YARN

DK weight (#3 Light).

Shown here: Alpaca with a Twist Baby Twist (100% alpaca; 110 yd [100 m]/50 g): #3008 Hot Flash, 5 balls.

NEEDLES

Size U.S. 6 (4 mm): 24" (60 cm) or longer circular (cir).

Adjust needle size if necessary to obtain the correct gauge.

NOTIONS

Tapestry needle.

GAUGE

19 stitches and 24 rows = 4" (10 cm) in stockinette stitch, before blocking.

This little semicircular shawl was inspired by crinkled Japanese maple (*palmatum*) leaves in autumn. The shawl decreases from the bottom edge up. The lace pattern incorporates the shaping, then concentric decreases are worked within the stockinette upper body. Blocking shows off the "crinkled" profile of the edging.

Notes

❧ This shawl begins at the bottom edge and decreases within the lace pattern. While working the first 42 rows of the chart, you'll decrease as follows: after Row 10, 325 stitches remain; after Row 26, 277 stitches remain; and after Row 38, 229 stitches remain.

❧ Patterning is worked on both right- and wrong-side rows. Follow the chart carefully.

Shawl

CO 373 sts. Work Rows 1–42 of Chart 1 once—229 sts rem (see Notes). Rep Rows 39–42 three times.

NEXT ROW: (RS) [K2, k2tog] twice, *[k1, k2tog] twice, k2, k2tog; rep from * to last st, k1—68 sts dec'd; 161 sts rem.

NEXT ROW: (WS) Purl.

Cont in St st for 10 rows more, ending with a WS row.

NEXT ROW: (RS) *K2, k2tog; rep from * to last st, k1—40 sts dec'd; 121 sts rem.

NEXT ROW: Purl.

Cont in St st for 10 rows more, ending with a WS row.

NEXT ROW: (RS) *K1, k2tog; rep from * to last st, k1—40 sts dec'd; 81 sts rem.

NEXT ROW: Purl.

Cont in St st for 10 rows more, ending with a WS row.

NEXT ROW: (RS) [K2tog] to last st, k1—40 sts dec'd; 41 sts rem.

NEXT ROW: Purl.

Cont in St st for 4 rows more, ending with a WS row.

NEXT ROW: [K2tog] to last st, k1—20 sts dec'd; 21 sts rem.

NEXT ROW: Purl.

Cont in St st for 2 rows more, ending with a WS row.

NEXT ROW: [K2tog] to last st, k1—10 sts dec'd; 11 sts rem.

NEXT ROW: Purl.

NEXT ROW: [K2tog] to last st, k1—6 sts rem.

NEXT ROW: (WS) [P2tog] 3 times—3 sts rem.

NEXT ROW: K3tog—1 st rem.

Fasten off last st.

Finishing

Weave in all ends. Block piece to finished measurements, pinning out the edging as shown in **figure 1** (opposite page).

Chart I

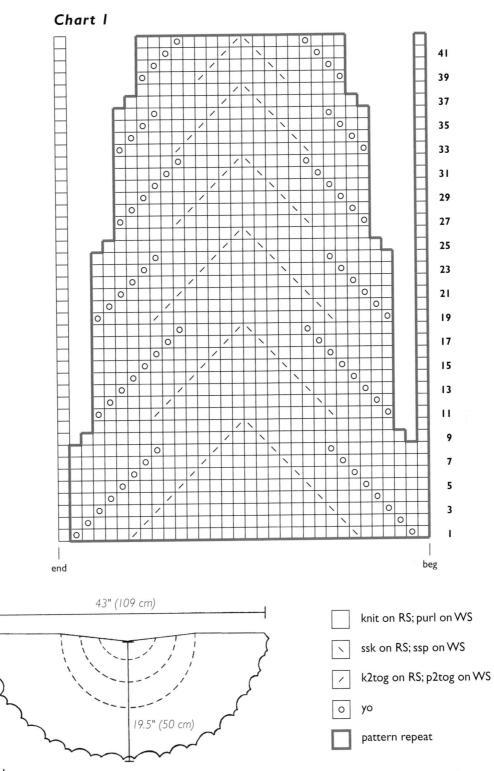

41
39
37
35
33
31
29
27
25
23
21
19
17
15
13
11
9
7
5
3
1

end   beg

43" (109 cm)

19.5" (50 cm)

Figure I

☐ knit on RS; purl on WS

╲ ssk on RS; ssp on WS

╱ k2tog on RS; p2tog on WS

○ yo

☐ pattern repeat

bethe

Angela Tong

FINISHED SIZE

About 50" (127 cm) wide and 12" (30.5 cm) deep, after blocking.

YARN

Fingering weight (#1 Super Fine).

Shown here: Lorna's Laces Shepherd Sock (80% wool, 20% nylon; 435 yd [398 m]/100 g): Manzanita, 1 skein.

NEEDLES

Size U.S. 6 (4 mm): 47" (120 cm) circular (cir).

Adjust needle size if necessary to obtain the correct gauge.

NOTIONS

Tapestry needle; blocking pins; blocking wires (optional).

GAUGE

19 stitches and 54 rows = 4" (10 cm) in garter stitch, blocked.

Traditional Shetland methods meet contemporary styling in a one-skein shawlette. The garter-stitch body is worked first, then stitches for the trellis border are picked up along the bottom edge. Finally, a knitted-on edging with petite bobbles creates interest.

- This shawl is made using the traditional Shetland construction method. See page 59 for more information on this method.

- The bobble edging is knitted on. You may find it easier to work with a double-pointed needle as the working needle for the edging.

STITCH GUIDE
Make Bobble (MB)

Work (k1, p1) 3 times into same st, sl first 5 sts on right-hand needle over 6th st.

Shawl
Garter-Stitch Body

Make a slipknot on needle—1 st.

ROW 1: Yo, k1—2 sts.

ROW 2: Yo, k2—3 sts.

ROW 3: Yo, k1, k1f&b, knit to end—2 sts inc'd.

Rep Row 3 every row 100 times—205 sts.

BO all sts loosely except for last st; do not break yarn. With 1 st on right needle, pick up, from back to front, the 104 yo loops along the curved edge of the shawl (do not knit any of these sts yet). Go back to the corner where the yarn is attached and knit across—105 sts.

NEXT ROW: (WS) Knit.

NEXT ROW: (RS) *K1, yo; rep from * to last st, k1—209 sts.

Trellis Lace Section

ROW 1: (WS) Purl.

ROW 2: (RS) K1, *yo, k2tog; rep from * to end.

ROW 3: (WS) Purl.

ROW 4: (RS) *Ssk, yo; rep from * to last st, k1.

ROWS 5–12: Rep Rows 1–4 two more times.

Garter Ridge

ROWS 13 AND 15: (WS) Purl.

ROWS 14 AND 16: (RS) Purl.

Rep Rows 1–12 of trellis lace section once more. Knit 2 rows.

Bobble Edging

NOTE: The edging will be joined to the body of the shawl at the end of Rows 2 and 4. The last k2tog includes 1 edging st and 1 body st.

With the yarn that is still attached to the body of the shawl, use the backward-loop method (see Techniques) to CO 6 sts. Turn work and knit back across 5 of the new sts, then k2tog (last st of edging will be joined to first st of the body of the shawl). Turn work and proceed with edging as foll:

ROW 1: K3, yo, k2tog, k1.

ROW 2: Sl 1 pwise, k2, yo, [k2tog] twice.

ROW 3: K3, yo, k2tog, k1.

ROW 4: MB (see Stitch Guide), k2, yo, [k2tog] twice.

Rep Rows 1–4 until only 6 edging sts rem. BO all sts.

Finishing

Weave in all ends. Wet-block piece to finished measurements using pins and blocking wires.

shetland construction

Method for Shawls

Angela Tong

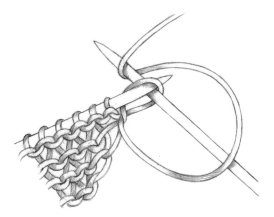

Figure 1
Working a yarnover at the beginning of a row.

This method for knitting shawls comes from the knitters of the Shetland Islands, off the northeast coast of Scotland. First, a short and wide garter-stitch triangle is worked from the bottom up, increasing at the edges. Yarnovers are worked at each edge (at the beginning of every row) to create the shaping; they also form visible loops along the edge of the shawl. Stitches are then picked up from these loops and a decorative border is worked outward from the triangle. The shawl is finished with an edging that is knitted back and forth or knitted on sideways and attached to the live stitches of the border.

The yarnovers in the garter-stitch body are worked as the first stitch of each row. To work a yarnover at the beginning of a row, bring your working yarn over the right needle from front to back, then knit the first stitch on the left needle (**figure 1**). The yarnover will make a loop sticking out from the right-hand side of the first knitted stitch (**figure 2**); be careful not to drop this loop when you work the following row.

The top, wide edge of the garter-stitch triangle is the bind-off edge. You should bind off loosely. Using an elastic bind-off will give you an elastic edge without requiring a change in your needle size. In her book *Wrapped in Lace* (Interweave, 2010), Margaret Stove recommends using the K2tog bind-off (see Techniques).

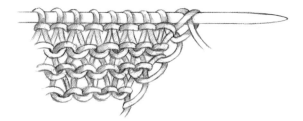

Figure 2
Several rows in garter stitch with yarnovers worked at the beginning of rows. Notice the open loops along the righthand edge; these are the yarnovers.

framework
Mercedes Tarasovich-Clark

FINISHED SIZE
About 47" (119.5 cm) wide at widest point of each segment and 15" (38 cm) deep from CO edge to BO points.

YARN
Fingering weight (#1 Super Fine).

Shown here: Quince and Co. Tern (75% wool, 25% silk; 221 yd [202 m]/50 g): #146 Kelp, 3 skeins.

NEEDLES
Size U.S. 8 (5 mm): 32" (80 cm) circular.

Adjust needle size if necessary to obtain the correct gauge.

NOTIONS
Markers (m); tapestry needle.

GAUGE
14 stitches and 18 rows = 4" (10 cm) in lace pattern stitch.

As she thought about classic triangular shawls, Mercedes Tarasovich-Clark wondered what could be added to or taken away from the shape to create something new. In this shawl, the triangle is both reduced, by casting on for flat-topped panels of lace, and expanded, by bringing in a third panel to make a longer wrap.

NOTE

❦ On each repeat of Row 25 of the Lace chart, the shawl will expand by 4 stitches in each segment, instead of the standard 2 stitches, to keep motifs aligned. On Row 47 of the chart, work [Stitches 1–17 as charted, repeat Stitches 4–17 eight more times, then work Stitches 40–55] in each section (ignore the gray-shaded portion, Stitches 18–39); 20 stitches are increased in each section across Row 47.

STITCH GUIDE

All RS rows

[K2, sl m, work charted patt to m, sl m] 3 times, k2.

All WS rows

[K2, sl m, work charted patt to m, sl m] 3 times, k2.

Shawl

CO 152 sts.

SET-UP ROW: [K2, place marker (pm), k48, pm] 3 times, k2.

Knit 3 rows.

Work Rows 1–12 of the Lace chart once, then Rows 7–12 four times—257 sts. Work Rows 13–24 of the Lace chart once, then Rows 25–34 twice—365 sts. Work Rows 35–48 of the Lace chart once—443 sts. Using the Decrease method (see Techniques), BO all sts.

Finishing

Weave in all ends. Block piece to finished measurements.

Lace

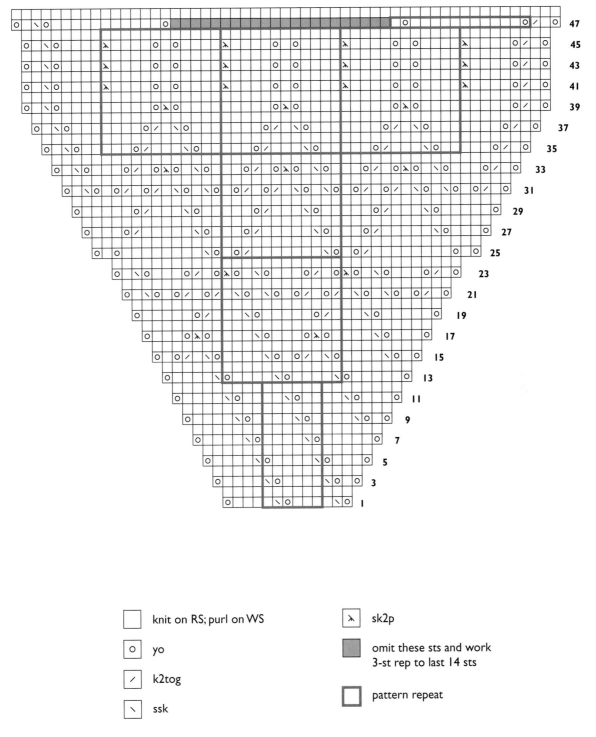

	knit on RS; purl on WS		sk2p
o	yo		omit these sts and work 3-st rep to last 14 sts
⁄	k2tog		pattern repeat
＼	ssk		

spathe

Heather Zoppetti

FINISHED SIZE

About 66" (167.5 cm) wide across top edge and 34" (86.5 cm) deep.

YARN

DK weight (#3 Light).

Shown here: Manos del Uruguay Silk Blend (70% merino, 30% silk; 150 yd [135 m]/50 g): #3206 Pine (green), 6 skeins.

Yarn distributed by Fairmount Fibers.

NEEDLES

Size U.S. 6 (4 mm): 32" (80 cm) or longer circular (cir).

Adjust needle size if necessary to obtain the correct gauge.

NOTIONS

Markers (m); tapestry needle.

GAUGE

20 stitches and 25 rows = 4" (10 cm) in lace pattern.

An epic shawl for the adventurer, this large triangle is knitted from the top down. Worked in a DK weight, it really doesn't require epic knitting, but you'll feel heroic wrapping this generous accessory around your shoulders.

NOTE

✿ This is a traditional top-down triangle. It begins with a tab foundation. See page 12 for tips on working this element.

Shawl

CO 3 sts. Knit 7 rows. With RS still facing, turn work 90 degrees clockwise and pick up and knit 3 sts along edge, then pick up and knit 3 sts along CO edge—9 sts.

ROW 1: (WS) K3, place marker (pm), [p1, pm] 3 times, k3.

ROW 2: (RS) Sl 1, k2, sl m, yo, k1, yo, sl m, k1, sl m, yo, k1, yo, sl m, k3—13 sts.

ROW 3: Sl 1, k2, purl to last 3 sts, k3.

ROW 4: Sl 1, k2, sl m, yo, k3, yo, sl m, k1, sl m, yo, k3, yo, sl m, k3—17 sts.

ROW 5: Sl 1, k2, purl to last 3 sts, k3.

Body

Work Rows 1–18 of Chart A once—57 sts. Work Rows 1–18 of Chart B 7 times, then rep Rows 1–16 once more—369 sts. Work Rows 1–20 of Chart C once—405 sts. Work Rows 1 and 2 of Chart D 4 times—405 sts. Using the Decrease method (see Techniques), BO all sts.

Finishing

Weave in all ends. Block piece to finished measurements.

Chart A

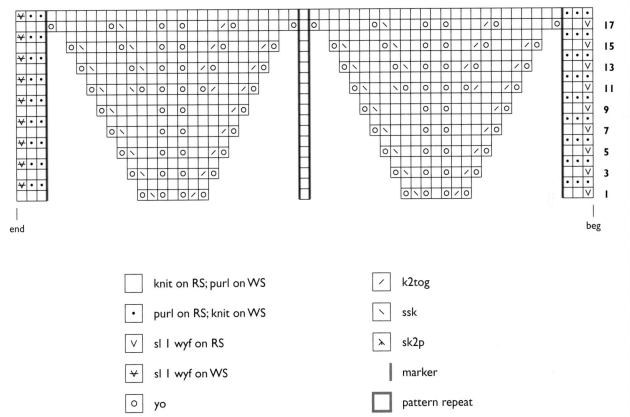

	knit on RS; purl on WS			/	k2tog
•	purl on RS; knit on WS			\	ssk
V	sl 1 wyf on RS			⅄	sk2p
⅄	sl 1 wyf on WS					marker
o	yo				pattern repeat

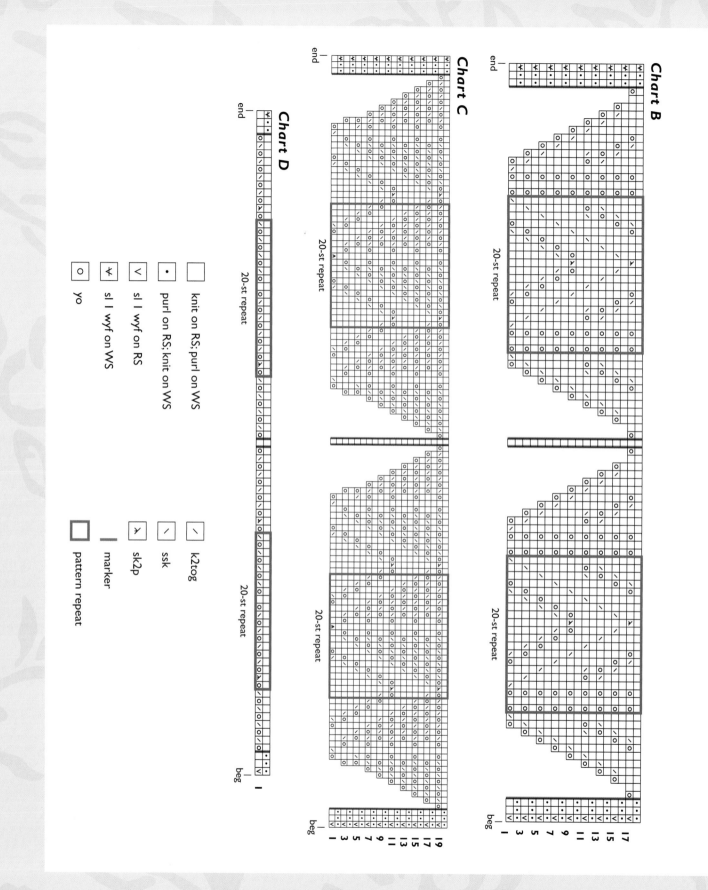

Chart B

Chart C

Chart D

20-st repeat

knit on RS; purl on WS

• purl on RS; knit on WS

∨ sl 1 wyf on RS

⋏ sl 1 wyf on WS

○ yo

＼ k2tog

／ ssk

⋏ sk2p

| marker

▢ pattern repeat

Chapter 5

simplicity

Simple styling and simple knitting lead to quick and quirky knits that anyone can tackle. Have fun with handpainted yarns, garter stitch, and innovative finishing tricks in these highly wearable shawls.

heath

Amy Gunderson

FINISHED SIZE

About 38" (96.5 cm) wide, 10" (25.5 cm) deep at center, and 3" (7.5 cm) deep at each end.

YARN

Fingering weight (#1 Super Fine).

Shown here: Noro Taiyo Sock (50% cotton, 17% wool, 17% nylon, 16% silk; 462 yd [422 m]/100g): #2 browns, greens, red, plum, 1 skein.

Yarn distributed by Knitting Fever.

NEEDLES

Size U.S. 6 (4 mm).

Adjust needle size if necessary to obtain the correct gauge.

NOTIONS

Markers (m); tapestry needle.

GAUGE

22 stitches and 28 rows = 4" (10 cm) in stockinette stitch; mesh edging measures 1¾" (4.5 cm) wide.

Garter stitch and dropped stitches make the most of self-striping sock yarn. The width of this sideways-knitted crescent melds perfectly with the yarn's color runs, which remind me of wildflowers on the English heath.

NOTES

❦ Stitch counts refer to the welted section only; stitch count in the lace edging does not change.

❦ All slipped stitches should be worked as follows: slip 1 purlwise with yarn in back (wyb).

❦ If you have a yarn scale, you can easily adapt this pattern to make the most of whatever yardage you have on hand. Before beginning, weigh your yarn. After the increase section is complete, weigh it again, making a note of how many grams you've used thus far. That amount is how much yarn you'll need to have left when beginning the decrease section.

STITCH GUIDE

Mesh Edging (worked over 11 sts)

ROW 1: P2, [k2tog, yo] 4 times, k1.

ROW 2: P1, [yo, p2tog] 4 times, k2.

Repeat Rows 1 and 2 for pattern.

Increase Half

CO 14 sts.

NEXT ROW: Sl 1 (see Notes), knit to end.

Garter-Stitch Increase Section

ROW 1: (RS) Work Row 1 of mesh edging (see Stitch Guide) over 11 sts, place marker (pm), M1L, knit to end—1 st inc'd.

ROW 2: (WS) Sl 1, knit to m, sl m, work Row 2 of mesh edging to end.

ROWS 3–6: Rep Rows 1 and 2 twice more—6 sts.

Short-Row Increase Section

Work in short-rows (see Techniques) as foll:

ROW 1: Work in patt to m, sl m, M1L, k4, wrap next st, turn.

ROW 2: Purl to m, sl m, work to end.

ROW 3: Work to m, sl m, M1L, k2, wrap next st, turn.

ROW 4: Purl to m, sl m, work to end.

ROW 5: Work to m, sl m, M1L, knit to end of row, hiding wraps.

ROW 6: Sl 1, k1, purl to m, sl m, work to end—9 sts.

Tier 2

Rep Rows 1–6 of garter-st inc section—12 sts. Rep Rows 1–6 of short-row inc section, except work Row 1 as k8 before turn, and Row 3 as k4 before turn—15 sts.

Tier 3

Rep Rows 1–6 of garter-st inc section—18 sts. Rep Rows 1–6 of short-row inc section, except work Row 1 as k12 before turn, and Row 3 as k6 before turn—21 sts.

Tier 4

Rep Rows 1–6 of garter-st inc section—24 sts. Rep Rows 1–6 of short-row inc section, except work Row 1 as k16 before turn, and Row 3 as k8 before turn—27 sts.

Tier 5

Rep Rows 1–6 of garter-st inc section—30 sts. Rep Rows 1–6 of short-row inc section, except work Row 1 as k20 before turn, and Row 3 as k10 before turn—33 sts.

Tier 6

Rep Rows 1–6 of garter-st inc section—36 sts. Rep Rows 1–6 of short-row inc section, except work Row 1 as k24 before turn, and Row 3 as k12 before turn—39 sts.

Tier 7

Rep Rows 1–6 of garter-st inc section—42 sts. Rep Rows 1–6 of short-row inc section, except work Row 1 as k28 before turn, and Row 3 as k14 before turn—45 sts.

Rep Rows 1–6 of garter-st inc section—48 sts.

Main Body

Short-Row Section

ROW 1: Work in patt to m, sl m, k32, wrap next st, turn.

ROW 2: Purl to m, sl m, work to end.

ROW 3: Work to m, sl m, k16, wrap next st, turn.

ROW 4: Purl to m, sl m, work to end.

ROW 5: Work to m, sl m, knit to end, hiding wraps.

ROW 6: Sl 1, k1, purl to m, sl m, work to end.

Garter-Stitch Section

ROW 1: Work to m, sl m, knit to end.

ROW 2: Sl 1, knit to m, sl m, work to end.

ROWS 3–6: Rep Rows 1 and 2 twice more.

Rep last 12 rows 26 more times, then work Rows 1–6 of short-row section once more.

Decrease Half

Garter-Stitch Decrease Section

ROW 1: Work to m, sl m, k2tog, knit to end—1 st dec'd.

ROW 2: Sl 1, knit to m, sl m, work to end.

ROWS 3–6: Rep Rows 1 and 2 twice more—45 sts.

Short-Row Decrease Section

ROW 1: Work to m, sl m, k2tog, k28, wrap next st, turn.

ROW 2: Purl to m, sl m, work to end.

ROW 3: Work to m, sl m, k2tog, k14, wrap next st, turn.

ROW 4: Purl to m, sl m, work to end.

ROW 5: Work to m, sl m, k2tog, knit to end, hiding wraps.

ROW 6: Sl 1, k1, purl to m, sl m, work to end—42 sts.

Tier 2

Rep Rows 1–6 of garter-st dec section—39 sts rem. Rep Rows 1–6 of short-row dec section, except work Row 1 as k24 before turn, and Row 3 as k12 before turn—36 sts rem.

Tier 3

Rep Rows 1–6 of garter-st dec section—33 sts rem. Rep Rows 1–6 of short-row dec section, except work Row 1 as k20 before turn, and Row 3 as k10 before turn—30 sts rem.

Tier 4

Rep Rows 1–6 of garter-st dec section—27 sts rem. Rep Rows 1–6 of short-row dec section, except work Row 1 as k16 before turn, and Row 3 as k8 before turn—24 sts rem.

Tier 5

Rep Rows 1–6 of garter-st dec section—21 st rem. Rep Rows 1–6 of short-row dec section, except work Row 1 as k12 before turn, and Row 3 as k6 before turn—18 sts rem.

Tier 6

Rep Rows 1–6 of garter-st dec section—15 sts rem. Rep Rows 1-6 of short-row dec section, except work Row 1 as k8 before turn, and Row 3 as k4 before turn—12 sts rem.

Tier 7

Rep Rows 1–6 of garter-st dec section—9 sts rem. Rep Rows 1–6 of short-row dec section, except work Row 1 as k4 before turn, and Row 3 as k2 before turn—6 sts rem. Rep Rows 1–6 of garter-st dec section—3 sts rem.

Knit 1 row. BO all sts.

Finishing

Weave in all ends. Block piece to finished measurements.

FINISHED SIZE

About 57" (145 cm) wide and 28½" (72.5 cm) deep.

YARN

Fingering weight (#1 Super Fine).

Shown here: Classic Elite Alpaca Sox (60% alpaca, 20% merino, 20% nylon; 450 yd [411 m]/100 g): #1809 Celadon (A) and #1884 Camo (B), 1 skein each.

NEEDLES

Size U.S. 4 (3.5 mm): 32" (80 cm) circular (cir).

Adjust needle size if necessary to obtain the correct gauge.

NOTIONS

Markers (m); tapestry needle.

GAUGE

18 stitches and 28 rows = 4" (10 cm) in stockinette stitch, after blocking.

bryusa
Alexandra Beck

Worked from the top down, this simple triangle features two-color slip-stitch patterning at the bottom edge. In an alpaca sock yarn, this accessory has a lovely halo.

STITCH GUIDE

I-cord Bind-off

Use the knitted method (see Techniques) to CO 3 sts at beg of row.

STEP 1: K2, k2togtbl (last st of I-cord with next st from shawl).

STEP 2: Sl 3 sts on right needle pwise with yarn in back (wyb) back to left needle.

STEP 3: Pulling yarn across the back of work, k2, k2togtbl (last st of I-cord with next st from shawl).

Rep Steps 2 and 3 until 3 I-cord sts rem, ending with Step 2.

STEP 4: Pulling yarn across back of work, k2tog, k1—2 sts rem.

STEP 5: Sl 2 sts on right needle pwise wyb back to left needle.

STEP 6: K2togtbl—1 st rem.

Break yarn and fasten off last st.

Shawl

Garter Tab

With A and using a provisional method (see Techniques), CO 3 sts.

ROWS 1–6: Knit.

ROW 7: Rotate piece 90 degrees clockwise and pick up and knit 3 sts along edge (1 st for each garter ridge), rotate piece 90 degrees clockwise, remove provisional CO, place 3 revealed sts on left needle, k3—9 sts. Cont with A.

ROW 8: (WS) K3, place marker (pm), [p1, pm] 3 times, k3.

ROW 9: (RS) K3, sl m, M1R, knit to next m, M1L, sl m, k1, sl m, M1R, knit to last m, M1L, sl m, k3—4 sts inc'd.

ROW 10 AND ALL WS ROWS: K3, purl to last 3 sts, k3.

Rep last 2 rows 49 more times, ending with Row 9—209 sts. Piece should measure about 15" (38 cm) from garter tab along center of shawl.

Slip-stitch section

ROW 1: (WS) With A, k3, sl m, p1, *k1, p1; rep from * to last m, sl m, k3.

ROW 2: (RS) With B, k3, sl m, M1R, k1, *sl 1, k1; rep from * to next m, M1L, sl m, k1, sl m, M1R, k1, *sl 1, k1; rep from * to last m, M1L, sl m, k3—4 sts inc'd.

ROW 3: With B, k3, sl m, p1, *k1, p1; rep from * to last m, sl m, k3.

ROW 4: (RS) With A, k3, sl m, M1R, k1, *sl 1, k1; rep from * to next m, M1L, sl m, k1, sl m, M1R, k1, *sl 1, k1; rep from * to last m, M1L, sl m, k3—4 sts inc'd.

Rep Rows 1–4 sixteen more times, then rep Rows 1–3 once more—349 sts. Piece should measure about 22½" (57 cm) from garter tab along center of shawl. With B, use the I-cord BO (see Stitch Guide) to BO all sts.

Finishing

Weave in all ends. Block piece to finished measurements.

lindsay
Tabetha Hedrick

FINISHED SIZE
About 77½" (197 cm) wide and 16" (40.5 cm) deep.

YARN
Fingering weight (#1 Super Fine).

Shown here: Shibui Knits Staccato (65% superwash merino, 30% silk, 5% nylon; 191 yd [175 m]/50 g): #115 Chrome (MC), 2 skeins; #165 Poodle Skirt (CC), 1 skein.

NEEDLES
Size U.S. 6 (4 mm): 24" (60 cm) circular (cir).

Adjust needle size if necessary to obtain the correct gauge.

NOTIONS
Tapestry needle.

GAUGE
16 stitches and 36 rows = 4" (10 cm) in stockinette stitch

Tabetha Hedrick was inspired by the legacy of pioneer women in the Rocky Mountains when she designed this shawl, which has a sweet, vintage appeal and streamlined patterning. Two colors of a sock yarn alternate within simple lace bands.

STITCH GUIDE
S5K
[Sl 1 st kwise] 4 times, k1, pass each slipped st over knitted st—4 sts dec'd.

Shawl

With MC, CO 363 sts. Work Rows 1–8 of the Lace chart once. Change to CC and work Rows 1–8 of the chart once more. Rep last 16 rows once more, changing colors with each 8-row rep. Change to MC and knit 4 rows, ending with a WS row. Work in short-rows without wrapping sts as foll:

NEXT ROW: (RS) K186, turn.

ROW 2: P9, turn.

ROW 3: K8, ssk, k3, turn—1 st dec'd.

ROW 4: P11, p2tog, p3, turn—1 st dec'd.

ROW 5: Knit to 1 st before last turn, ssk, k3, turn—1 st dec'd.

ROW 6: Purl to 1 st before last turn, p2tog, p3, turn—1 st dec'd.

Rep last 2 rows 36 more times—25 sts rem on each side outside turning points.

ROW 1: (RS) Knit to 1 st before last turn, ssk, k4, turn—1 st dec'd.

ROW 2: (WS) Purl to 1 st before last turn, p2tog, p4, turn—1 st dec'd.

Rep last 2 rows 4 more times—277 sts rem. Change to CC and knit 5 rows. BO all sts loosely.

Finishing

Weave in all ends. Block piece to finished measurements.

Lace

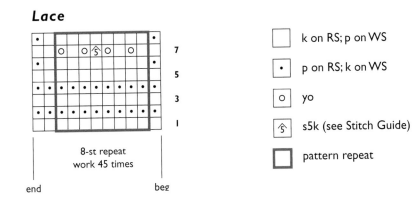

☐	k on RS; p on WS
•	p on RS; k on WS
○	yo
ⓢ	s5k (see Stitch Guide)
☐	pattern repeat

8-st repeat
work 45 times

end   beg

7

5

3

1

maedwe

AnneLena Mattison

FINISHED SIZE

About 82" (208 cm) wide and 10"
(25.5 cm) deep.

YARN

Fingering weight (#1 Super Fine).

Shown here: Shalimar Yarns Breathless (75%
merino, 15% cashmere, 10% silk; 420 yd
[384 m]/100 g): Sprout, 1 skein.

NEEDLES

Size U.S. 6 (4 mm): 24" (60 cm) circular
(cir).

Adjust needle size if necessary to obtain
the correct gauge.

NOTIONS

Markers (m); tapestry needle.

GAUGE

25½ stitches and 24 rows = 4" (10 cm) in
garter stitch after blocking.

Pull out that precious skein of luxury
sock yarn—Maedwe is the perfect
project for it. Garter-stitch fabric is
edged with short-row ruffles for a
simple, striking accessory. AnneLena also
provides tips for adjusting the pattern, in
case you don't quite have 420 yards, or
if you want to use your own handspun.

❦ This shawlette makes a great one-skein project using sock yarn. If you are a spinner or using yarn that comes with more or less yardage than the recommended yarn, you can adjust the pattern to suit your yarn. Weigh your skein before beginning. Cast on and work the increase rows until you have used 49 percent of the yarn, ending with Row 24, then begin working the decrease rows. This way, you will use your yarn most effectively, though the shawlette may be a different size.

Shawlette

CO 11 sts.

Increase rows

Work in short-rows (see Techniques) as follows:

ROW 1: K1, place marker (pm), k10.

ROW 2: Sl 1 with yarn in front (wyf), p8, wrap next st, turn.

ROW 3: K9.

ROW 4: Sl 1 wyf, p9, sl m, k1.

ROW 5: K1, sl m, p9, k1.

ROW 6: Sl 1 wyf, k8, wrap next st, turn.

ROW 7: P8, k1.

ROW 8: Sl 1 wyf, k9, sl m, k1.

ROW 9: K1f&b, sl m, k10—1 st inc'd.

ROW 10: Sl 1 wyf, p8, wrap next st, turn.

ROW 11: K9.

ROW 12: Sl 1 wyf, p9, sl m, k2.

ROW 13: K2, sl m, p9, k1.

ROW 14: Sl 1 wyf, k8, wrap next st, turn.

ROW 15: P8, k1.

ROW 16: Sl 1 wyf, k9, sl m, k2.

ROW 17: Knit to 1 st before m, k1f&b, sl m, k10—1 st inc'd.

ROW 18: Sl 1 wyf, p8, wrap next st, turn.

ROW 19: K9.

ROW 20: Sl 1 wyf, p9, sl m, knit to end.

ROW 21: Knit to m, sl m, p9, k1.

ROW 22: Sl 1 wyf, k8, wrap next st, turn.

ROW 23: P8, k1.

ROW 24: Sl 1 wyf, k9, sl m, knit to end.

Rep Rows 17–24 fifty-one more times, ending with Row 24—64 sts (see sidebar if adjusting pattern for yarn amount).

Decrease rows

ROW 1: Knit to 2 st before m, k2tog, sl m, k10—1 st dec'd.

ROW 2: Sl 1 wyf, p8, wrap next st, turn.

ROW 3: K9.

ROW 4: Sl 1 wyf, p9, sl m, knit to end.

ROW 5: Knit to m, sl m, p9, k1.

ROW 6: Sl 1 wyf, k8, wrap next st, turn.

ROW 7: P8, k1.

ROW 8: Sl 1 wyf, k9, sl m, knit to end.

Rep Rows 1–8 fifty-two more times, ending with Row 8—11 sts rem. BO all sts.

Finishing

Weave in all ends. Block piece to finished measurements.

elven

Angela Tong

FINISHED SIZE

About 49" (124.5 cm) wide and 15½" (39.5 cm) deep, after blocking.

YARN

Fingering weight (#1 Super Fine).

Shown here: Schoppel Wolle Zauberball (75% wool, 25% nylon; 459 yd [420 m]/100 g): #1966 Summer Meadow, 1 skein. Yarn distributed by Skacel.

NEEDLES

Size U.S. 6 (4 mm): 40" (100 cm) circular.

Adjust needle size if necessary to obtain the correct gauge.

NOTIONS

Markers (m); stitch holder; tapestry needle; blocking pins.

GAUGE

24 stitches and 46 rows = 4" (10 cm) in garter stitch, blocked.

Elongated wings make this shawl easy to wear. A leaf motif edges a stockinette border, all worked in a self-striping sock yarn. A variegated yarn would make for an entirely different look, but because of the design's simplicity, it's well-suited to handpainted yarns.

Double Decrease (DD)

Sl 2 sts tog as if to k2tog, k1, pass 2 slipped sts over—2 sts dec'd.

Sk2p

Sl 1 pwise, k2tog, pass slipped st over—2 sts dec'd.

Shawl

CO 22 sts, leaving a 6" (15 cm) tail for grafting.

ROW 1: (WS) P10, place marker (pm), yo, k2, yo, pm, p10—24 sts.

ROW 2: (RS) K6, DD (see Stitch Guide), yo, k1, yo, sl m, k4, sl m, yo, k1, yo, sk2p (see Stitch Guide), k6.

ROW 3: (WS) P10, sl m, yo, k4, yo, sl m, p10—26 sts.

ROW 4: (RS) K4, DD, k1, [yo, k1] 2 times, sl m, k6, sl m, k1, [yo, k1] 2 times, sk2p, k4.

ROW 5: (WS) P10, sl m yo, k6, yo, sl m, p10—28 sts.

ROW 6: (RS) K2, DD, k2, yo, k1, yo, k2, sl m, k8, sl m, k2, yo, k1, yo, k2, sk2p, k2.

ROW 7: (WS) P10, sl m, yo, k8, yo, sl m, p10—30 sts.

ROW 8: (RS) DD, k3, yo, k1, yo, k3, sl m, k10, sl m, k3, yo, k1, yo, k3, sk2p.

Body

ROW 1: (WS) P10, sl m, yo, knit to m, yo, sl m, p10—2 sts inc'd.

ROW 2: (RS) K6, DD, yo, k1, yo, sl m, knit to m, sl m, yo, k1, yo, sk2p, k6.

ROW 3: (WS) P10, sl m, yo, knit to m, yo, sl m, p10—2 sts inc'd.

ROW 4: (RS) K4, DD, k1, [yo, k1] 2 times, sl m, knit to m, sl m, k1, [yo, k1] 2 times, sk2p, k4.

ROW 5: (WS) P10, sl m yo, knit to m, yo, sl m, p10—2 sts inc'd.

ROW 6: (RS) K2, DD, k2, yo, k1, yo, k2, sl m, knit to m, sl m, k2, yo, k1, yo, k2, sk2p, k2.

ROW 7: (WS) P10, sl m, yo, knit to m, yo, sl m, p10—2 sts inc'd.

ROW 8: (RS) DD, k3, yo, k1, yo, k3, sl m, knit to m, sl m, k3, yo, k1, yo, k3, sk2p.

Rep last 8 rows 18 more times—182 sts.

Split

NEXT ROW: (WS) P10, sl m, yo, k50, place the 61 sts just worked on a holder, BO next 62 sts loosely, knit to m, yo, sl m, p10—61 sts rem each side.

Right Side

ROW 1: (RS) K6, DD, yo, k1, yo, sl m, knit to last 4 sts, k3tog, k1—2 sts dec'd.

ROW 2: (WS) Knit to m, yo, sl m, p10—1 st inc'd.

ROW 3: (RS) K4, DD, k1, [yo, k1] 2 times, knit to last 4 sts, k3tog, k1—2 sts dec'd.

ROW 4: (WS) Knit to m, yo, sl m, p10—1 st inc'd.

ROW 5: (RS) K2, DD, k2, yo, k1, yo, k2, sl m, knit to last 4 sts, k3tog, k1—2 sts dec'd.

ROW 6: (WS) Knit to m, yo, sl m, p10—1 st inc'd.

ROW 7: (RS) DD, k3, yo, k1, yo, k3, sl m, knit to last 4 sts, k3tog, k1—2 sts dec'd.

ROW 8: (WS) Knit to m, yo, sl m, p10—1 st inc'd.

Rep last 8 rows 10 more times—17 sts rem. Work Rows 1–7 once more—12 sts rem. BO sts kwise. Cut yarn leaving a 4" (10 cm) tail.

Left Side

Transfer 61 held sts to needle. Join yarn with RS facing.

ROW 1: (RS) K1, sssk (see Techniques), knit to m, sl m, yo, k1, yo, sk2p, k6—2 sts dec'd.

ROW 2: (WS) P10, sl m, yo, knit to end—1 st inc'd.

ROW 3: (RS) K1, sssk, knit to m, sl m, k1, [yo, k1] 2 times, sk2p, k4—2 sts dec'd.

ROW 4: (WS) P10, sl m, yo, knit to end—1 st inc'd.

ROW 5: (RS) K1, sssk, knit to m, sl m, k2, yo, k1, yo, k2, sk2p, k2—2 sts dec'd.

ROW 6: (WS) P10, sl m, yo, knit to end—1 st inc'd.

ROW 7: (RS) K1, sssk, knit to m, sl m, k3, yo, k1, yo, k3, sk2p—2 sts dec'd.

ROW 8: (WS) P10, sl m, yo, knit to end—1 st inc'd.

Rep last 8 rows 10 more times—17 sts rem. Work Rows 1–7 once more—12 sts rem. BO sts kwise. Cut yarn.

Finishing

Thread tail from CO onto tapestry needle. Graft the ends of the leaf edging together with Kitchener st (see Techniques). Weave in all ends. Wet-block piece to finished measurements, using pins to block out the leaf edging.

rhoeas

Mercedes Tarasovich-Clark

FINISHED SIZE

About 76" (193 cm) wide and 18" (45.5 cm) deep, not including fringe.

YARN

Worsted weight (#4 Medium).

Shown here: Spud & Chloë Sweater (55% superwash wool, 45% organic cotton; 160 yd [146 m]/100 g): #7501 Popsicle, 4 skeins.

NEEDLES

Size U.S. 9 (5.5 mm): 24" (60 cm) circular (cir).

Adjust needle size if necessary to obtain the correct gauge.

NOTIONS

Markers (m); tapestry needle.

GAUGE

15 stitches and 27 rows = 4" (10 cm) in garter stitch.

Horseshoe lace edges a generous garter-stitch triangle. Worked in a worsted wool-cotton blend on size U.S. 9 (5.5 mm) needles, the knitting goes quickly and makes a large, lofty accessory. Self-fringe makes for faster finishing—see the designer's tutorial on this technique on page 99.

Shawl

CO 9 sts.

Set up

ROW 1: (WS) K1, place marker (pm), p1, pm, k2, pm, p5.

ROW 2: (RS) K5, sl m, k2, lifted inc right slant (see Techniques), k1, sl m, M1, k1—2 sts inc'd.

ROW 3 AND ALL WS ROWS: Knit to m, sl m, purl to m, sl m, k2, sl m, p5.

ROW 4: K5, sl m, k2, sl m, lifted inc right slant, knit to m, sl m, knit to end—1 st inc'd.

ROW 6: K5, sl m, k2, sl m, lifted inc right slant, knit to m, sl m, M1, knit to end—2 sts inc'd.

ROWS 8–17: Work Rows 4–7 twice more, then Rows 4–5 once more—21 sts. '

On last row, remove second and third markers, leaving the first marker between garter sts and lace patt—16 sts in lace section and 5 sts in garter st section.

Body

NEXT ROW: Work Lace Edging chart over 16 sts, sl m, knit to end.

Work 1 more row in patt, working edging sts according to chart.

Increases

INC ROW: (RS) Work the Lace Edging chart to m, sl m, M1, knit to end—1 st inc'd.

Work Inc row every 4th row 53 more times—75 sts; piece should measure about 37" (94 cm) from bottom. Work even in patt for 8 rows.

Decreases

DEC ROW: (RS) Work Lace Edging chart to m, sl m, k2tog, knit to end—1 st dec'd.

Work Dec row every 4th row 53 more times, ending with a WS row—21 sts rem.

End Shawl

ROW 1: (RS) K5, pm, k2, pm, ssk, knit to m, sl m, knit to end—1 st dec'd.

ROW 2 AND ALL WS ROWS: Knit to m, sl m, purl to m, sl m, k2, sl m, p5.

ROW 3: K5, sl m, k2, sl m, ssk, knit to m, sl m, k2tog, knit to end—2 sts dec'd.

ROWS 5–18: Work Rows 1–4 twice more then Rows 1–2 once more—11 sts rem.

ROW 19: (RS) K5, sl m, k2, remove m, ssk, remove m, k2tog—9 sts rem.

ROW 20: P2, k2, sl m, p5.

BO AND SET UP FRINGE: (RS) K5, remove m, BO 4 rem sts. Drop 5 rem sts from needle and let them ravel down to CO edge.

Finishing

Finish fringe as directed on page 99. Weave in all ends. Block piece to finished measurements.

Lace Edging

			o	⋏	o			•	•							5
		o		⋏		o			•		•					3
o			⋏			o		•		•						1

16 sts

☐ knit on RS; purl on WS

• purl on RS; knit on WS

o yo

⋏ sk2p

☐ pattern repeat

Creating A Self-Fringing
knitted edge
Mercedes Tarasovich-Clark

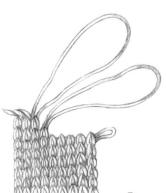

Figure 1

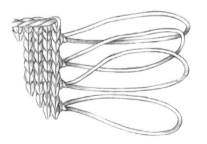

Figure 2

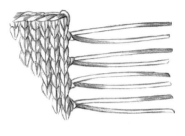

Figure 3

Making fringe can be tedious. Cutting and attaching individual pieces of yarn to a project can take forever. An easy solution is to take advantage of knitted fabric's natural ability to unravel, and knit the fringe as you go! By leaving a margin of plain fabric on the edge of a knitted shape, you can create attached fringe of any length. The loose stitches will unravel lengthwise, but won't unravel widthwise.

This method works especially well for shawls that are worked side to side, such as Rhoeas (shown at left), because the selvedge edge becomes the bottom edge when the shawl is worn. You could also work self-fringe as part of a knitted-on edging.

Begin by determining how many stitches you need to work to create the fringe length you want. Once the stitches are unraveled, how long is the strand of yarn that remains (**figure 1**)? A good rule of thumb is to knit a margin about one-third of the final fringe length, but this can vary with yarn thickness and individual knitters' gauge, so be sure to swatch. Once you determine how many stitches you need to achieve your desired fringe length, add this number to your cast-on number and work the extra stitches in plain stockinette at the outer edge of the project.

Once you've finished knitting your project, bind off all EXCEPT the fringe stitches. Slip your needle out of the fringe stitches. *Use your fingers or a knitting needle to tease apart the first two rows of stitches, resulting in a loose loop of yarn. Tie this loop off with an overhand knot, close to the fabric edge (**figure 2**). Repeat from * for every fringe loop, ending with your cast-on edge loop.

The resulting fringe will be crinkled and kinked, so you'll need to give it a good steaming. Your secret weapon? A fork! Use a metal fork to keep the fringe loops under slight tension as you hover your iron over the loops, letting them straighten out under the steam. You can then leave your fringe looped or trim each loop to create traditional fringe (**figure 3**).

texture

Cables, knit-purl combinations, and rustic textures create cozy wraps. This collection of shawl designs shows off the possibilities of side-to-side construction and some innovative shapes.

Carol Feller

FINISHED SIZE

About 45" (114.5 cm) wide and 20" (51 cm) deep at edge.

YARN

Worsted weight (#4 Medium).

Shown here: Berroco Ultra Alpaca (50% alpaca, 50% wool; 215 yd [198 m]/100 g): #6208 Couscous, 3 skeins.

NEEDLES

Size U.S. 9 (5.5 mm): 40" (100 cm) circular (cir).

Size U.S. 8 (5 mm): 40" (100 cm) cir.

Adjust needle size if necessary to obtain the correct gauge.

NOTIONS

Removable marker (m), tapestry needle.

GAUGE

16 stitches and 26 rows = 4" (10 cm) in stockinette stitch on smaller needles; 16 stitches and 33 rows = 4" (10 cm) in garter stitch on smaller needles.

Use the magic of short-rows to create triangles and curves within a rectangular shawl. Worked in a worsted-weight alpaca, this shawl is about bundling up and getting warm while showing off a modern, geometric sensibility.

STITCH GUIDE

I-cord Bind-Off

At beg of row, use knitted method to CO 3 sts, *k2, ssk (last I-cord st with next shawl st), place all 3 sts back on left needle and rep from * until all shawl sts have been worked—3 I-cord sts rem on needle. K3tog, break yarn, and fasten off rem st.

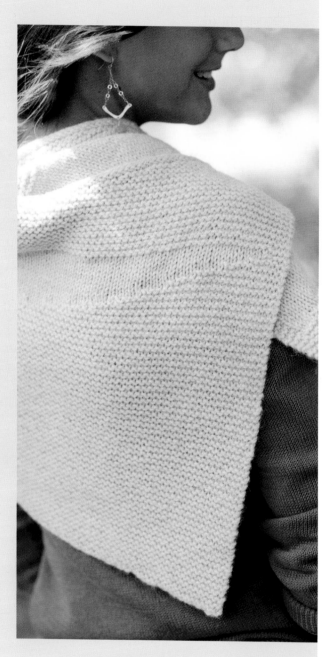

Shawl

With larger cir needle, CO 180 sts.

NEXT ROW: With smaller cir needle, sl 1 kwise, knit to end.

Rep last row on every row until piece measures 1½" (3.8 cm) from CO. Work in short-rows (see Techniques) as foll:

SHORT-ROW I: (RS) Sl 1 kwise, knit to last 4 sts, wrap next st, turn.

NEXT ROW: (WS) Knit to end of row.

SHORT-ROW 2: (RS) Sl 1 kwise, knit to 4 sts before previously wrapped st, wrap next st, turn.

NOTE: It can be helpful to use a removable marker to mark the turning point, and then move it to the new position on the next row.

Cont to work WS return row and Short-row 2 until all sts have been worked. Work 1 more WS row.

NEXT ROW: (RS) Sl 1, knit to end of row, hiding wraps.

SHORT-ROW 3: (WS) Sl 1, k2, p2, wrap next st, turn.

NEXT ROW: (RS) Knit to end of row.

SHORT-ROW 4: (WS) Sl 1, k2, purl to previously wrapped st, purl st with wrap, p4, wrap next st, turn.

Cont to work RS return row and Short-row 4 until all sts have been worked. Work 1 more RS row.

NEXT ROW: Sl 1 kwise, knit to end of row.

Rep last row 2 more times.

Right Curved Edge

SHORT-ROW I: (RS) Sl 1 kwise, k85, wrap next st, turn.

All WS rows: Knit to end.

SHORT-ROW 2: (RS) Sl 1 kwise, knit to 7 sts before previously wrapped st, wrap next st, turn.

Rep Short-row 2 on foll RS row—71 sts rem in work.

SHORT-ROW 3: (RS) Sl 1 kwise, knit to 6 sts before previously wrapped st, wrap next st, turn. Rep Short-row 3 on foll 2 RS rows—53 sts rem in work.

SHORT-ROW 4: (RS) Sl 1 kwise, knit to 5 sts before previously wrapped st, wrap next st, turn.

Rep Short-row 4 on foll 3 RS rows—33 sts rem in work.

SHORT-ROW 5: (RS) Sl 1 kwise, knit to 4 sts before previously wrapped st, wrap next st, turn. Rep Short-row 5 on foll 2 RS rows—21 sts rem in work.

SHORT-ROW 6: (RS) Sl 1 kwise, knit to 3 sts before previously wrapped st, wrap next st, turn. Rep Short-row 6 on foll 3 RS rows—9 sts rem in work.

SHORT-ROW 7: (RS) Sl 1 kwise, knit to 2 sts before previously wrapped st, wrap next st, turn. Rep Short-row 7 on foll RS row—5 sts rem in work.

SHORT-ROW 8: (RS) Sl 1 kwise, knit to 1 st before previously wrapped st, wrap next st, turn. Rep Short-row 8 on foll 3 RS rows—1 st rem in work. Work 1 more WS row.

NEXT ROW: (RS) Sl 1, knit to end.

Left Curved Edge

SHORT-ROW 1: (WS) Sl 1 kwise, k85, wrap next st, turn.

ALL RS ROWS: Knit to end.

SHORT-ROW 2: (WS) Sl 1 kwise, knit to 7 sts before previously wrapped st, wrap next st, turn. Rep Short-row 2 on foll WS row—71 sts rem in work.

SHORT-ROW 3: (WS) Sl 1 kwise, knit to 6 sts before previously wrapped st, wrap next st, turn. Rep Short-row 3 on foll 2 WS rows—53 sts rem in work.

SHORT-ROW 4: (WS) Sl 1 kwise, knit to 5 sts before previously wrapped st, wrap next st, turn. Rep Short-row 4 on foll 3 WS rows—33 sts rem in work.

SHORT-ROW 5: (WS) Sl 1 kwise, knit to 4 sts before previously wrapped st, wrap next st, turn. Rep Short-row 5 on foll 2 WS rows—21 sts rem in work.

SHORT-ROW 6: (WS) Sl 1 kwise, knit to 3 sts before previously wrapped st, wrap next st, turn. Rep Short-row 6 on foll 3 WS rows—9 sts rem in work.

SHORT-ROW 7: (WS) Sl 1 kwise, knit to 2 sts before previously wrapped st, wrap next st, turn. Rep Short-row 7 on foll WS row—5 sts rem in work.

SHORT-ROW 8: (WS) Sl 1 kwise, knit to 1 st before previously wrapped st, wrap next st, turn. Rep Short-row 8 on foll 3 WS rows—1 st rem in work. Work 1 more WS row.

NEXT ROW: (WS) Sl 1, knit to end.

BO all sts using I-cord BO (see Stitch Guide).

Finishing

Block piece to finished measurements.

fauve
Kyoko Nakayoshi

FINISHED SIZE
About 52¾" (134 cm) wide and 22¾" (58 cm) deep, not including bobbles.

YARN
Aran weight (#4 Medium).

Shown here: Artesano Aran (50% alpaca, 50% wool; 144 yd [132 m]/100 g): #CA03 Maple, 5 skeins.

NEEDLES
Size U.S. 8 (5 mm): 24" (60 cm) circular (cir).

Adjust needle size if necessary to obtain the correct gauge.

NOTIONS
Tapestry needle; size G/6 (4 mm) crochet hook; cable needle (cn).

GAUGE
23 stitches and 22 rows = 4" (10 cm) in pattern stitch (blocked).

A trapezoid shape is knitted from the top down in sections. Kyoko used large cable motifs in a chunky-weight yarn to create drama. Achieved with crochet techniques, the unusual bobble edging creates a playful yet elegant finish.

Notes

❦ The shawl is comprised of three triangles. On the chart, work the first section twice for the first two segments of the shawl, then the second section once for the third segment.

❦ As you work the rows, each triangle increases in width. After the 54th row, repeat the section within the red lines one additional time for each repeat of Rows 19–54 to complete each triangle.

❦ The bobble edge is worked using a crochet hook. The trick is to make individual loops slightly loose (the same length as the chain stitches) to get the puffy bobble look.

❦ If your tension is especially loose, then it's best to bind off a couple of rows sooner than the instructions indicate to make sure you have enough yarn left.

STITCH GUIDE

2/1 RC (2 over 1 Right Cross)
Sl 1 st to cn and hold in back, k2, k1 from cn.

2/1 LC (2 over 1 Left Cross)
Sl 2 sts to cn and hold in front, k1, k2 from cn.

2/2 LC (2 over 2 Left Cross)
Sl 2 sts to cn and hold in front, k2, k2 from cn.

2/1 RPC (2 over 1 Right Purl Cross)
Sl 1 st to cn and hold in back, k2, p1 from cn.

2/1 LPC (2 over 1 Left Purl Cross)
Sl 2 sts to cn and hold in front, p1, k2 from cn.

Bobble Edging (multiple of 3 sts)
See Techniques for crochet instructions.

*With crochet hook, ch 3, [yo, insert hook into same st and draw a loop] 4 times, yo, draw a loop through all loops on hook, skip 2 sts, insert hook into the 3rd st, yo and draw through loop on hook, pull yarn to tighten; rep from * to end.

Shawl

CO 4 sts.

PREPARATION ROW 1: (RS) *(K1, yo, k1) into same st, ([k1, yo] twice, k1) all in next st; rep from * once more—16 sts.

PREPARATION ROWS 2, 4 AND 6: (WS) Purl.

PREPARATION ROW 3: *2/2 LC (see Stitch Guide), yo; rep from * twice more, 2/2 LC—19 sts.

PREPARATION ROW 5: *K5, yo; rep from * twice more, k4—22 sts.

PREPARATION ROW 7: *K4, yo, k2, yo: rep from * twice more, k4—28 sts.

PREPARATION ROW 8: Purl.

Work Rows 1–54 of Chart 1 once—208 sts.

ROWS 55 TO 90: Rep Rows 19–54 of Chart 1 once more—328 sts.

ROWS 91 TO 107: Rep Rows 19–35 of Chart 1—388 sts.

NEXT ROW: (WS) BO all sts except for last st—1 st rem.

Edging

Transfer rem st onto a crochet hook. Work bobble edging (see Stitch Guide) to end.

Cut yarn and pull.

Finishing

You can adjust the bobbles by pulling the sts forward using the tip of the knitting needle to make the shawl puffy on the RS. Weave in all ends. Block piece to finished measurements.

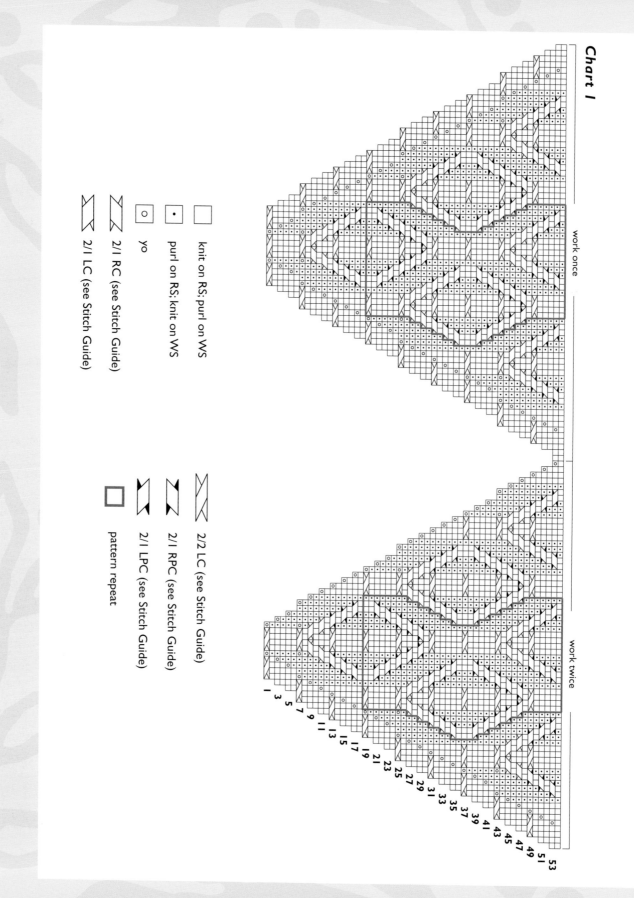

Chart I

Legend:

☐ knit on RS; purl on WS

• purl on RS; knit on WS

◯ yo

2/1 LC (see Stitch Guide)

2/1 RC (see Stitch Guide)

2/2 LC (see Stitch Guide)

2/1 RPC (see Stitch Guide)

2/1 LPC (see Stitch Guide)

☐ pattern repeat

work once

work twice

glen lennox

Kate Gagnon Osborn

FINISHED SIZE
About 55" (139.5 cm) wide and 16½" (42 cm) deep.

YARN
Worsted weight (#4 Medium).

Shown here: The Fibre Company Organik (70% organic merino, 15% alpaca, 15% silk; 98 yd [89m]/50g): Arctic Tundra, 4 skeins.

NEEDLES
Size U.S. 8 (5 mm): 24" (60 cm) circular (cir).

Adjust needle size if necessary to obtain the correct gauge.

NOTIONS
Tapestry needle; cable needle (cn).

GAUGE
15½ stitches and 25 rows = 4" (10 cm) in seed stitch.

Worked in a luxurious worsted weight, this simple triangle has lovely drape and coziness. Shaping occurs inside the cabled edge, increasing from one corner to the midpoint, then decreasing to the other end.

🌿 This shawl is worked sideways from corner to corner. The interior is worked in seed stitch. The red lines on the charts indicate the seed-stitch repeat.

STITCH GUIDE

3/3 RC (3 over 3 Right Cross)

Sl 3 sts to cn and hold in back, k3, k3 from cn.

2/3 RC (2 over 3 Right Cross)

Sl 3 sts to cn and hold in back, k2, k3 from cn.

Shawl

CO 6 sts.

Set up

ROW 1: (RS) Sl 1, k2, M1, k3—7 sts.

ROW 2: (WS) Sl 3 sts pwise with yarn in front (wyf), purl to end.

ROW 3: Sl 1, k2, M1, k4—8 sts.

ROWS 4, 6, AND 8: Rep Row 2.

ROW 5: Sl 1, k2, M1, k5—9 sts.

ROW 7: 3/3 RC, k3.

ROW 9: Sl 1, k5, M1, k3—10 sts.

ROW 10: Sl 3 sts pwise wyf, k1, p6.

ROW 11: Sl 1, k5, M1, knit to end—11 sts.

ROW 12: Sl 3 sts pwise wyf, k1, p7.

ROW 13: Sl 1, k5, M1, p1, k4—12 sts.

ROW 14: Sl 3 sts pwise wyf, k1, p1, k1, p6.

Body

Work Rows 1–6 of the Increase chart 28 times—68 sts. Work Rows 1 and 2 of the Increase chart once more. Work Rows 1–6 of the Decrease chart 28 times—12 sts rem.

Ending

ROW 1: (RS) Sl 1, k4, sl 1, k1, psso, p1, k4—11 sts rem.

ROW 2: (WS) Sl 3 sts pwise wyf, k1, p7.

ROW 3: Sl 1, k4, sl 1, k1, psso, k4—10 sts rem.

ROW 4: Sl 3 sts pwise wyf, p7.

ROW 5: 3/3 RC, k4.

ROW 6: Rep Row 4.

ROW 7: Sl 1, k4, sl 1, k1, psso, k3—9 sts rem.

ROW 8: Sl 3 sts pwise wyf, p6.

ROW 9: Sl 1, k3, k2tog, k3—8 sts rem.

ROW 10: Sl 3 sts pwise wyf, p5.

ROW 11: 2/3 RC, k3.

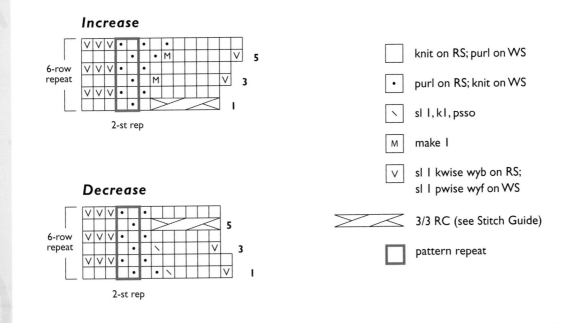

Increase

6-row repeat

2-st rep

Decrease

6-row repeat

2-st rep

	knit on RS; purl on WS
•	purl on RS; knit on WS
＼	sl 1, k1, psso
M	make 1
V	sl 1 kwise wyb on RS; sl 1 pwise wyf on WS
⧓	3/3 RC (see Stitch Guide)
☐	pattern repeat

ROW 12: Rep Row 10.

ROW 13: Sl 1, k2, k2tog, k3—7 sts rem.

ROW 14: Sl 3 sts pwise wyf, p4.

ROW 15: Sl 1, k1, k2tog, k3—6 sts rem.

BO all sts pwise on WS.

Finishing

Weave in all ends. Block piece to finished measurements.

the return journey

Lisa Shroyer

FINISHED SIZE

About 84" (213.5 cm) long and 14"
(35.5 cm) deep at center.

YARN

Worsted weight (#4 Medium).

Shown here: Plymouth Worsted Merino
Superwash (100% merino; 218 yd
[199 m]/100 g): #7 Heather Gray, 4 skeins.

NEEDLES

Size U.S. 7 (4.5 mm): 24" (60 cm) or
longer circular (cir).

Adjust needle size if necessary to obtain
the correct gauge.

NOTIONS

Waste yarn for provisional cast-on; tapestry needle; cable needle (cn).

GAUGE

15 stitches of charted pattern repeat = 2½"
(6.5 cm) wide; 29 rows in pattern = 4"
(10 cm) high.

The best adventures aren't just about
arriving—but about making your way
back as well. This cabled shawl starts at
one corner and is worked side to side,
increasing, then decreasing, at a slow rate,
which creates a long, shallow triangle.
I-cord edges are worked in as you go.
When you arrive at the end, finishing is
minimal—the journey is complete!

NOTES

❦ This shawl is worked side to side and features shaping along the right-hand edge to create a triangle.

❦ The edges are worked in a three-stitch I-cord pattern. These stitches are not shown on the charts, but the edge pattern should be worked throughout.

STITCH GUIDE

I-cord Edging (worked over 3 sts at each edge)

ROW 1: (RS) With yarn held in back (wyb), sl 3 sts pwise; pull yarn taut across WS and work in patt to last 3 sts, k3.

ROW 2: (WS) With yarn held in front (wyf), sl 3 sts pwise; pull yarn taut across front of work and work in patt to last 3 sts, p3.

Rep Rows 1 and 2 throughout for patt.

1/1 LC (1 over 1 Left Cross)

Sl 1 to cn and hold in front, k1 tbl, k1 tbl from cn.

1/1 RC (1 over 1 Right Cross)

Sl 1 to cn and hold in back, k1 tbl, k1 tbl from cn.

1/1 LPC (1 over 1 Left Purl Cross)

Sl 1 to cn and hold in front, p1, k1 tbl from cn.

1/1 RPC (1 over 1 Right Purl Cross)

Sl 1 to cn and hold in back, k1 tbl, p1 from cn.

2/2 LPC (2 over 2 Left Purl Cross)

Sl 2 to cn and hold in front, (k1 tbl) twice, sl sts on cn to left needle tip, sl knit st from left needle tip to cn and hold in front, p1 from left needle, k1 tbl from cn.

2/2 RPC (2 over 2 Right Purl Cross)

Sl 2 to cn and hold in back, sl purl st on left needle tip to right needle tip, then to right needle tip of cn, k1 tbl from left needle, (p1, [k1 tbl] twice) from cn.

1/2 LPC dec (1 over 2 Left Purl Cross Decrease)

Sl 1 to right needle tip, sl 1 to cn and hold in front, sl st from right needle tip back to left needle tip, p2tog, k1 tbl from cn.

Shawl

Use the invisible provisional method (see Techniques) to CO 3 sts. Work 4 rows in I-cord (see Techniques).

NEXT ROW: With RS still facing, turn work 90 degrees clockwise and use right needle tip to pick up and knit 3 sts along side of I-cord; carefully remove waste yarn from CO and place 3 live sts on left needle, then knit these 3 sts—9 sts total.

NEXT ROW: (WS) P3, work Row 1 of Chart A over 3 sts, p3.

NEXT ROW: (RS) Work 3 sts in I-cord edging patt (see Stitch Guide), work Row 2 of Chart A, work last 3 sts in I-cord edging patt.

NEXT ROW: (WS) Work 3 sts in edging patt, work Row 3 of chart, work 3 sts in edging patt.

Cont to work edge sts in patt (see Notes) and work in charted patt through Row 63—24 sts total; 6 edge sts + 18 body sts. Work Rows 64–123 four times, working full reps according to red rep box—84 sts: 6 edge sts + 78 body sts; piece should measure about 42" (106.5 cm) from bottom.

Shape second half

Work Rows 1–60 of Chart B four times, working full reps according to red rep box—24 sts rem: 6 edge sts + 18 body sts. Work Rows 61–120 once—9 sts rem: 6 edge sts + 3 body sts.

NEXT ROW: (RS) Sl 3 sts wyb, k3tog, sl 4 sts back to left needle, pull yarn taut across WS, k2, ssk, sl 3 sts back to left needle, *k3, sl 3 sts back to left needle and pull yarn taut across WS; rep from * once more—6 sts rem.

Break the yarn and thread the tail onto the tapestry needle. Arrange sts on needle tips—3 sts each tip—and, with RS facing, use Kitchener st (see Techniques) to graft edges together.

Finishing

Weave in all ends. Block piece to finished measurements.

Chart A

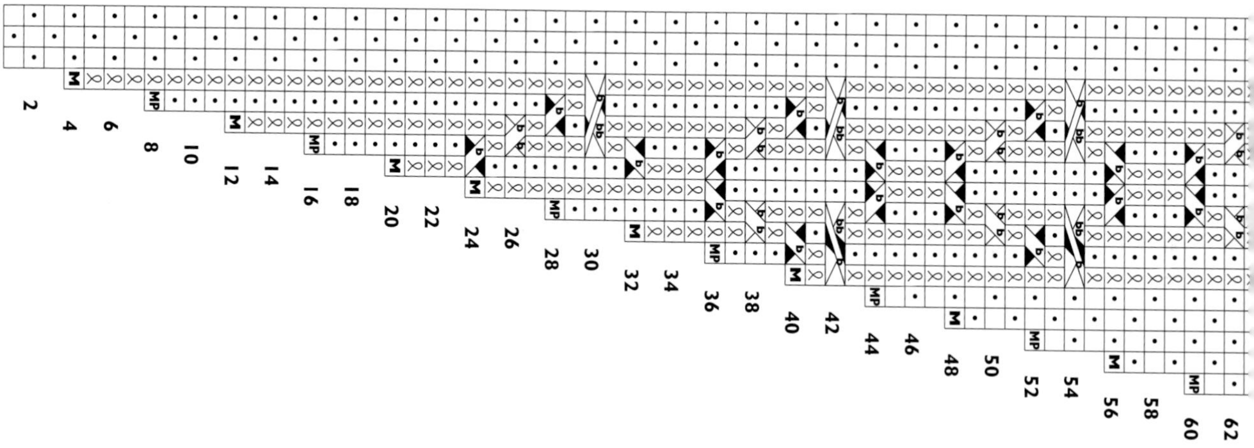
2 4 6 8 10 12 14 16 18 20 22 24 26 28 30 32 34 36 38 40 42 44 46 48 50 52 54 56 58 60 62

Chart B

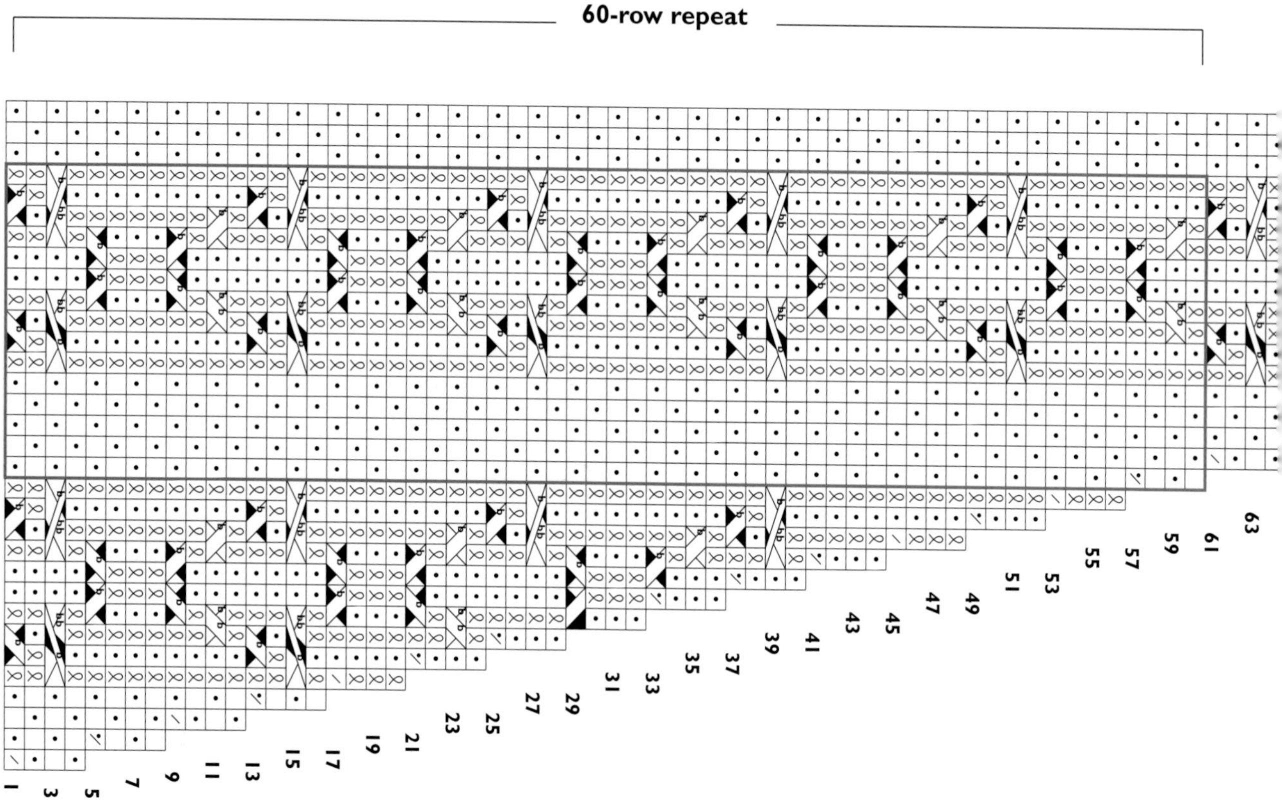
60-row repeat
1 3 5 7 9 11 13 15 17 19 21 23 25 27 29 31 33 35 37 39 41 43 45 47 49 51 53 55 57 59 61 63

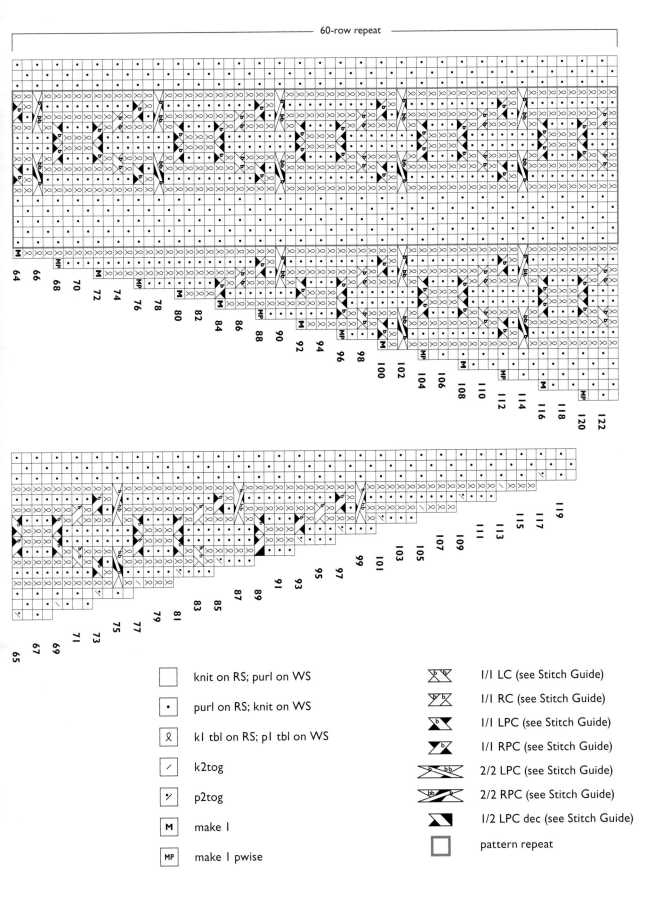

knit on RS; purl on WS

· purl on RS; knit on WS

ℛ k1 tbl on RS; p1 tbl on WS

╱ k2tog

╲ p2tog

M make 1

MP make 1 pwise

1/1 LC (see Stitch Guide)

1/1 RC (see Stitch Guide)

1/1 LPC (see Stitch Guide)

1/1 RPC (see Stitch Guide)

2/2 LPC (see Stitch Guide)

2/2 RPC (see Stitch Guide)

1/2 LPC dec (see Stitch Guide)

pattern repeat

glossary

In the following section you will find the tools and resources you need to carry out special techniques, purchase yarns, and find out more about the designers of these wonderful pieces.

Abbreviations

beg(s) begin(s); beginning

CC contrast color

cm centimeters

cn cable needle

CO cast on

cont continue(s); continuing

dec(s) decrease(s); decreasing

foll follow(s); following

g gram(s)

inc(s) increase(s); increasing

k knit

k1f&b knit into the front and back of the same stitch

kwise knitwise, as if to knit

k2tog knit 2 sts together

k*tbl knit [designated number of stitches] through the back loop

m marker(s)

MC main color

mm millimeter(s)

M1L make 1 left: From the front, insert left needle tip under the horizontal bar between two stitches and lift it. Knit the lifted loop through the back loop (1 st inc'd).

M1R make 1 right: From the back, insert left needle tip under the horizontal bar between two stitches and lift it. Knit into the lifted loop (1 st inc'd).

p purl

p1f&b purl into the front and back of the same stitch

p2tog purl 2 stitches together

patt pattern(s)

pm place marker

psso pass slipped stitch over

pwise purlwise, as if to purl

rem remain(s); remaining

rep repeat(s); repeating

RS right side

sk2p Sl 1 purlwise, k2tog, pass slipped st over—2 sts dec'd.

sl slip

sl m slip marker

sl st slip stitch (slip 1 stitch purlwise unless otherwise indicated)

ssk slip slip knit ([slip 1 stitch knitwise] 2 times, knit slipped sts tog through back loops)

st(s) stitch(es)

tbl through the back loop

tog together

WS wrong side

wyb with yarn in back

wyf with yarn in front

yo yarnover

* repeat starting point

** repeat all instructions between asterisks

() alternate measurements and/or instructions

[] work instructions as a group a specified number of times

Techniques

Cast-ons
Backward-Loop Cast-On

*Loop working yarn and place on needle backward so that it doesn't unwind. Repeat from * for desired number of stitches.

Crochet Chain (Provisional) Cast-On

With waste yarn and crochet hook, make a loose crochet chain (see page 130) about four stitches more than you need to cast on. With needle, working yarn, and beginning two stitches from end of chain, pick up and knit one stitch through the back loop of each crochet chain *(figure 1)* for desired number of stitches. When you're ready to work in the opposite direction, pull out the crochet chain to expose live stitches *(figure 2)*.

Figure 1

Figure 2

Invisible (Provisional) Cast-On

Place a loose slipknot on the needle held in your right hand. Hold waste yarn next to slipknot and around your left thumb; hold working yarn over your left index finger. *Bring needle forward under waste yarn, over working yarn, grab a loop of working yarn *(figure 1)*, then bring needle to the front, over both yarns, and grab a second loop *(figure 2)*. Repeat from * for desired number of stitches. When you're ready to work in the opposite direction, carefully remove waste yarn to expose live stitches.

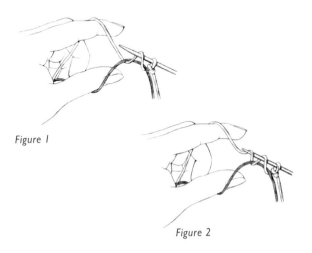

Figure 1

Figure 2

Knitted Cast-On

Make a slipknot of working yarn and place it on the left needle if there are no stitches already there. *Use the right needle to knit the first stitch (or slipknot) on left needle *(figure 1)* and place new loop onto left needle to form a new stitch *(figure 2)*. Repeat from * for the desired number of stitches, always working into the last stitch made.

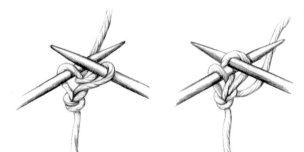

Figure 1   Figure 2

Bind-Offs
Decrease Bind-Off
Version A: Knitting through the back loops

This version gives a bind-off edge that looks just like a standard bind-off, but it is much stretchier.

STEP 1: Knit together the first two stitches on the left needle through the back loop *(figure 1)*.

STEP 2: Slip the new stitch on the right needle back to the left needle *(figure 2)*.

STEP 3: Repeat 1 and 2 until all stitches are bound off.

Notice how the bind-off edge is nearly indistiguishable from your normal bind-off, but give it a tug and you'll see how much more flexible it is.

Version B: Knitting through the front loops

STEP 1: Knit together the first two stitches on the left needle *(figure 3)*.

STEP 2: Slip the new stitch on the right needle back to the left needle.

STEP 3: Repeat these two steps until all stitches are bound off.

Here, contrasting color yarn is used in the bind-off row so you can see the finished effect more clearly.

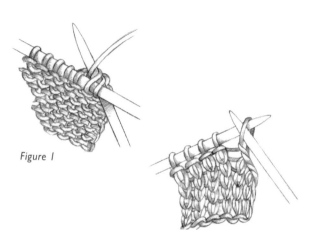

Figure 1

Figure 2

Figure 3

Figure 4

I-Cord Bind-Off

With right side facing and using the knitted method, cast on three stitches (for cord) onto the end of the needle holding the stitches to be bound off *(figure 1)*, *k2, k2tog through back loops (the last cord stitch with the first stitch to be bound off; *(figure 2)*, slip these three stitches back to the left needle *(figure 3)*, and pull the yarn firmly from the back. Repeat from * until three stitches remain on left needle and no stitches remain on right needle. Bind off remaining stitches using the standard method.

Figure 1

Figure 2

Figure 3

K2tog Bind-Off

This bind-off gives a very elastic edge without needing to change needle size or tension.

K2, *slip both sts back to left needle, k2togtbl, k1, rep from * until all sts are BO.

How to Work a Short-Row

Work to turn point, slip next stitch purlwise to right needle. Bring yarn to front *(figure 1)*. Slip same stitch back to left needle *(figure 2)*. Turn work and bring yarn in position for next stitch, wrapping the slipped stitch as you do so.

NOTE: Hide wraps on a knit stitch when right side of piece is worked as a knit stitch. Leave wrap if the purl stitch shows on the right side. Hide wraps as follows:

KNIT STITCH: On right side, work to just before wrapped stitch, insert right needle from front, under the wrap from bottom up, and then into wrapped stitch as usual. Knit them together, making sure the new stitch comes out under wrap.

PURL STITCH: On wrong side, work to just before wrapped stitch. Insert right needle from back, under wrap from bottom up, and put on left needle. Purl lifted wrap and stitch together.

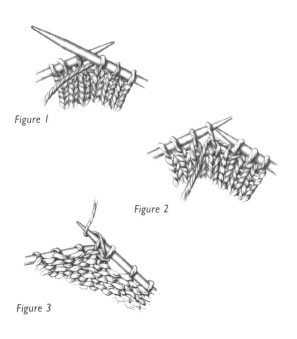
Figure 1

Figure 2

Figure 3

Lifted Increase (LI)

RIGHT SLANT (RLI): Knit into the back of the stitch (in the "purl bump") in the row directly below the "first stitch on the left needle *(figure 1)*, then knit the stitch on the needle *(figure 2)* and slip the original stitch off the needle.

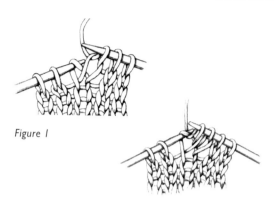

Figure 1

Figure 2

Duplicate Stitch

Duplicate Stitch on Stockinette Stitch

Horizontal: Bring threaded needle out from back to front at the base of the V of the knitted stitch you want to cover. *Working right to left, pass needle in and out under the stitch in the row above it and back into the base of the same stitch. Bring needle back out at the base of the V of the next stitch to the left. Repeat from *.

Vertical: Beginning at lowest point, work as for horizontal duplicate stitch, ending by bringing the needle back out at the base of the stitch directly above the stitch just worked.

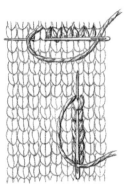

Duplicate Stitch on Reverse Stockinette Stitch

Thread yarn to be woven in on tapestry needle. Working from right to left, insert tapestry needle up into a purl bump. *Following the path of the underlying stitch, insert needle into the next purl bump to the upper right of first bump *(figure 1)*. Continue following the path of the yarn and, bringing needle down, insert needle down into next purl bump to the left, then back down through the first purl bump *(figure 2)*. Follow the path of the yarn and insert needle up through the next purl bump to the left, then repeat from *.

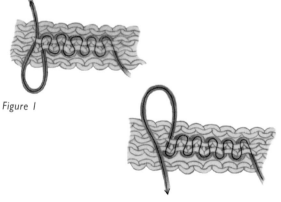

Figure 1

Figure 2

Duplicate Stitch on Garter Stitch

Thread yarn to be woven in on tapestry needle. Working from right to left, insert needle up through a purl bump *(figure 1)*. *Following the path of the underlying stitch, bring needle down through next purl bump to the left *(figure 2)*. Spread garter-stitch fabric out and find the stockinette row below the purl bump you're working on. Insert needle from right to left under the legs of the knit stitch below last purl bump entered *(figure 3)*. Bring needle up and insert needle back up through last purl bump entered. Repeat from *.

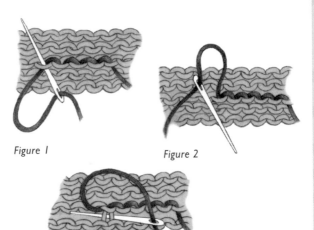

Figure 1   Figure 2

Figure 3

Emily Ocker Circular Beginning

This method for casting on for a circle in the round is invisible. Leaving a tail, make a large loop with the yarn. Hold the loop so that the crossing area of the loop is on the top and the tail is off to the left. With a double-pointed knitting needle, *reach inside the loop and pull the yarn coming from the ball through to make a stitch, then take the needle up over the top of the loop and yarn over; repeat from * until you have the desired number of stitches on the needle. Turn and knit one row. If you're casting on an even number of stitches, the sequence ends with a yarnover, and it will be difficult to keep from losing the last stitch. To solve this, pick up 1 extra stitch from the inside and then work these last 2 stitches together on the first row to get back to an even number of stitches. Divide the stitches evenly onto four double-pointed needles.

I-Cord

With double-pointed needle, cast on desired number of stitches (three stitches shown here). *Without turning the needle, slide the stitches to the other point, pull yarn around the back, and knit the stitches as usual. Repeat from * for desired length.

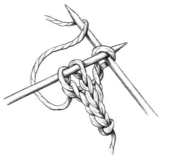

Crochet Chain

Make a slipknot and place on crochet hook. *Yarn over hook and draw it through loop of the slipknot. Repeat from *, drawing yarn through loop on hook, for desired length. To fasten off, cut yarn and draw tail through last loop formed.

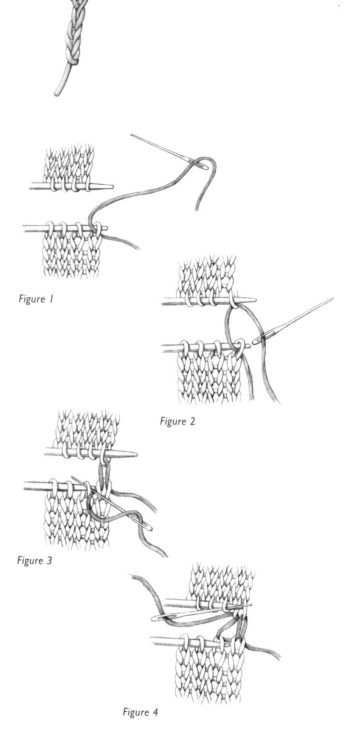

Kitchener Stitch

STEP 1: Bring tapestry needle through the first stitch on the front needle as if to purl and leave the stitch on the needle (figure 1).

STEP 2: Bring tapestry needle through the first stitch on the back needle as if to knit and leave that stitch on the needle (figure 2).

STEP 3: Bring tapestry needle through the first front stitch as if to knit and slip this stitch off the needle, then bring the tapestry needle through the next front stitch as if to purl and leave this stitch on the needle (figure 3).

STEP 4: Bring tapestry needle through the first back stitch as if to purl and slip this stitch off the needle, then bring the tapestry needle through the next back stitch as if to knit and leave this stitch on the needle (figure 4).

Repeat Steps 3 and 4 until 1 stitch remains on each needle, adjusting the tension to match the rest of the knitting as you go. To finish, bring the tapestry needle through the front stitch as if to knit and slip this stitch off the needle, then bring the tapestry needle through the back stitch as if to purl and slip this stitch off the needle.

Insert the tapestry needle into the center of the last stitch worked, pull the yarn to the wrong side, and weave the tail into the purl bumps on the wrong side of the toe.

Figure 1

Figure 2

Figure 3

Figure 4

sources for yarns

Alpaca with a Twist
4272 Evans Jacobi Rd.
Georgetown, IN 47122
(866) 37-TWIST [378-9478]
alpacawithatwist.com

Anzula Luxury Fibers
anzula.com

Artesano Ltd.
Unit G, Lamb's Farm Business Park
Basingstoke Rd., Swallowfield
Reading, Berkshire
England RG7 1PQ
+44 (0)118 9503350
artesanoyarns.co.uk

Berroco Inc.
1 Tupperware Dr., Ste. 4
North Smithfield, RI 02896
(401) 769-1212
berroco.com

**Blue Sky Alpacas/
Spud & Chloë**
PO Box 88
Cedar, MN 55011
(763) 753-5815
blueskyalpacas.com

Brooklyn Tweed
brooklyntweed.net

Classic Elite Yarns
122 Western Ave.
Lowell, MA, 01851
(978) 453-2837
classiceliteyarns.com

Claudia Hand Painted Yarns
(540) 433-1140
claudiaco.com

**Fairmount Fibers/
Manos del Uruguay**
915 N. 28th St.
Philadelphia, PA, 19130
(888) 566-9970
fairmountfibers.com

Hazel Knits
hazelknits.com

**Kelbourne Woolens/
The Fibre Company**
2000 Manor Rd.
Conshohocken, PA 19428
(484) 368-3666
kelbournewoolens.com

Knitting Fever/Noro
PO Box 336
Amityville, NY 11701
(516) 546-3600
knittingfever.com

Lorna's Laces
4229 N. Honore St.
Chicago, IL 60613
(773) 935-3803
lornaslaces.net

Louet North America
3425 Hands Rd.
Prescott, ON
Canada K0E 1T0
(800) 897-6444
louet.com

Quince and Co.
(877) 309-6762
quinceandco.com

Shibui Knits
1101 SW Alder St.
Portland, OR 97205
(503) 595-5898
shibuiknits.com

**Skacel Collection/
Schoppel Wolle**
PO Box 88110
Seattle, WA 98138
(800) 255-1278
skacelknitting.com

for further reading

Bush, Nancy. *Knitted Lace of Estonia*. Loveland, CO: Interweave, 2010.

Johnson, Wendy D. *Wendy Knits Lace: Essential Techniques and Patterns for Irresistible Everyday Lace*. New York: Potter Craft, 2011.

Moss, Jean. *Sweet Shawlettes: 25 Irresistible Patterns for Knitting Cowls, Capelets, and More*. Newtown, CT: Taunton, 2012.

Noble, Carol Rasmussen. *Knits from the North Sea: Lace in the Shetland Tradition*. Bothell, WA: Martingale & Co, 2009.

Oberle, Cheryl. *Folk Shawls: 25 Knitting Patterns and Tales from Around the World*. Loveland, CO: Interweave, 2000.

Stove, Margaret. *Wrapped in Lace: Knitted Heirloom Designs from Around the World*. Loveland, CO: Interweave, 2010.

Thies, Sheryl. *Nature's Wrapture: Contemporary Knitted Shawls*. Bothell, WA: Martingale & Co, 2010.

Waterman, Martha. *Traditional Knitted and Lace Shawls*. St. Paul, MN: Dos Tejedoras, 1993.

——. *Traditional Knitted Lace Shawls*. Loveland, CO: Interweave, 1998.

about the designers

Alexandra Beck is a knitwear designer based in Stuttgart, Germany. You can find more of her work at alexandstacey.wordpress.com.

After her work day at NASA is over, *Hilary Smith Callis* spends her evenings designing knitwear at her home in San Francisco. She combines her fiber-related pursuits with her previous life as a student of Classics at theyarniad.com.

Carol Feller is a knitwear designer and teacher in Ireland. She is author of *Contemporary Irish Knits* (Wiley, 2011), and she self-publishes patterns at stolenstitches.com.

Melissa J. Goodale designs as Stick Chick Knits in Seattle, Washington. You can find her online at scknits.com and on Twitter @scknits.

Amy Gunderson lives in North Carolina and can be found online at getoffmylawndesigns.com.

Tabetha Hedrick is a designer in Colorado. For more information, visit tabethahedrick.com.

Rosemary (Romi) Hill is a designer in California. Her successful lace collections have earned her a large following. You can check them out at designsbyromi.com.

Maura Kirk is a trapeze artist in Philadelphia, who also works in the yarn industry. You can find her online at theprojectoryhandcrafts.com.

AnneLena Mattison lives in Northern California with her husband and their six kids. She not only knits and designs, but also spins and weaves.

Kyoko Nakayoshi is a Japanese designer and pattern translator living in London. You can find more of her work at cottonandcloud.com.

Kate Gagnon Osborn is co-owner of Kelbourne Woolens, distributor of The Fibre Company's yarns. Her designs have appeared in many publications, including two books she co-authored with Courtney Kelley, *Vintage Modern Knits* (Interweave, 2011) and *November Knits* (Interweave, 2012).

Besides writing knitting books, *Lisa Shroyer* writes poetry and designs Fair Isle projects at home in Chapel Hill, North Carolina.

Mercedes Tarasovich-Clark knits, designs, and writes outside of Birmingham, Alabama. Visit her on the Web at mercedesknits.com.

Angela Tong is a knit and crochet designer in Brooklyn, New York. She is as passionate about crafting as she is about food. Follow her crafting and cooking adventures at oiyi.blogspot.com.

Alexis Winslow lives in Brooklyn, New York, and works as a printed textile designer. As co-founder of the philanthropic organization CharitySub.org, she believes that with a bit of patience and work, we can all make a difference in this world. Her website is knitdarling.com.

Heather Zoppetti lives in Lancaster, Pennsylvania. You can learn more about her work at digitalnabi.com.

index

Knit *shawls* & *wraps* for every day with more inspiration from Interweave!

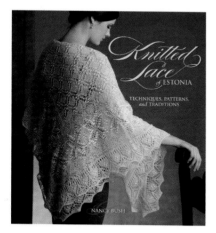

Knitted Lace of Estonia
Techniques, Patterns, and Traditions
Nancy Bush
ISBN 978-1-59668-315-0
$26.95

A Knitting Wrapsody with DVD
Innovative Designs to Wrap, Drape, and Tie
Kristin Omdahl
ISBN 978-1-59668-307-5
$24.95

Wrapped in Lace
Knitted Heirloom Designs from Around the World
Margaret Stove
ISBN 978-1-59668-227-6
$26.95

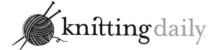